Kenzie on Lincolnshire fields in 1950.
Photo courtesy Bob Ashby.

Kenzie

Kenzie
THE WILD-GOOSE MAN

COLIN WILLOCK

Illustrated by
Mackenzie Thorpe and John Lathey
and with photographs

COCH-Y-BONDDU BOOKS
2018

First published by Andre Deutsch, 1962
Reprinted 1972, 1975, 1977
Second edition, The Country Book Club, 1972
Third edition, Boydell Country Library paperback, 1985
Fourth edition, Tideline Books, 1997

This (Fifth) edition, Coch-y-Bonddu Books, 2018

ISBN 978 1 904784 89 0

© Executors of Colin Dennistoun Willock and Coch-y-Bonddu Books Ltd. 2018

Cover image: USFWS Mountain-Prairie (Pintails & Mallards) [CC BY 2.0 (https://creativecommons.org/licenses/by/2.0)], via Wikimedia Commons

Coch-y-Bonddu Books Ltd, Machynlleth, Powys SY20 8DG
01654 702837
www.anglebooks.com

All rights reserved. No part of this publication may be reproduced, stored in a retrieval system, or transmitted, in any form or by any means, electronic, mechanical, photocopying, recording or otherwise, without the prior consent of the copyright holder.

Printed and bound in Great Britain by TJ International Ltd

For Gordon and May

List of Illustrations

Frontispiece of Kenzie in 1950.	
Map of the Wash.	24–25
A nice morning's bag.	34
Kenzie at his easel, finishing a painting.	50
A snapshot of Bob Ashby and Kenzie, 1950.	70
Kenzie at his easel in the 1950s.	89
Kenzie's wildfowl drawings.	104–107
Kenzie at his houseboat.	124
Kenzie's houseboat.	137
Kenzie making a brew.	150
Kenzie scanning the winter fields.	167

Foreword

I count myself very lucky that my early wildfowling career coincided with the lives of some of the great characters of the salt marsh, men whose like we are probably not going to see again. Ted Eales, for one, warden of the National Trust Nature Reserve at Blakeney Point. Ted had been brought up with a gun in one hand and binoculars in the other. Billy Bishop, warden just down the coast at the Norfolk Naturalist's Trust reserve at Cley was of exactly the same stamp. Like Ted, he was a brilliant instinctive naturalist and shot. And, of course, I must include the only surviving member of the trio, Stratton Long, punt-gunner, and close fowling friend of both.

This trio of marshland heroes were all what you might call 'legit'. Though none of them was above knocking off the odd pheasant that had strayed too far from its home ground. None-the-less they operated very much within the law. The fourth great character, the subject of this book, sometimes did not, at least not until the closing stages of his career and there must even be a faint doubt about that.

It is not pure chance that all four great fowlers came from East Anglia. The coast of the eastern counties seems to grow larger-than-life characters as easily as its saltings grow samphire and sea lavender. The sea is in their blood. After all, Nelson drew many of his crews from Blakeney and the surrounding villages. I only hope it will continue to produce such men, though circumstances are changing so fast that I fear the day of the buccaneer is over.

But I must concentrate on Kenzie. My first contact with him was back in the 'fifties. I paid him a modest fee to take me out on the Wash sands, as he had guided hundreds of others, to try to bag my first goose. I didn't succeed. Kenzie called and shot the only goose of the flight. I had learned the first lesson of life with Kenzie. Wyatt Earp could have told me. It was: draw fast and shoot first! As a result of this encounter I wrote a piece about Kenzie for the *Observer* magazine. Andre Deutsch, my then publisher, saw it, and with his partner, the famous artist and cartoonist, Nicholas Bentley, took off for Sutton

Bridge in Lincolnshire, to meet Kenzie in person. I can think of no more unlikely meeting. Andre had probably only seen the sea at Cap d'Antibes and Nick had certainly never sullied his immaculate shoes with marsh mud. They were, however, both deeply impressed—as I had been—with the character of the man more formally known as Mackenzie Thorpe. They phoned me on their return to London demanding that I write a book about him. This is it—and I can't say how delighted I am that it is once again available. I immodestly believe in years to come that it will be regarded as a source book about certain—largely illegal—aspects of rural England in the 'thirties and 'forties and wildfowling as it once was.

Kenzie and I soon became close friends. Naturally, I made as many fowling trips as possible for 'research purposes'. However, these could never provide one hundredth of the rich background, let alone the deep wildfowl and wildlife knowledge, of the old rogue and so some other system of communication had to be devised.

This, as it turned out, was simplicity itself. Kenzie had recently acquired a fairly basic tape recorder. He swore that this was for the purpose of recording the calls of geese and wigeon in the wild. Possibly so, but I am fairly sure that its real purpose was to play back the recordings to call the fowl within shot. If so, Kenzie was wasting his time since he could already call anything from pinkfeet to golden plover to hares. He certainly didn't need any electronic aids. However, I may be doing him an injustice. He was, like all the best wildfowlers, deeply interested in his quarry, its calls, its migratory habits and its behaviour. As an illustration of this concern, at the back of his council house at Sutton Bridge he kept a miniature Wildfowl Trust consisting of wounded birds that he or other fowlers had pricked and which he devotedly nursed back to health. Such is the ambivalence of all true wildfowlers!

The tape recorder produced a stream of information, which I played and replayed until I knew most of it by heart. If I had queries—and there were lots of them—I sent my questions on tape and usually received a reply by return. Then I indexed every story, every poaching foray, every aspect of Kenzie's remarkable life until I felt I was ready to start selecting and putting it down on paper. And if I did succeed in capturing the essence of the man it must have been because I heard his voice inside my head even as I wrote. To this day my wife, who knew and liked Kenzie almost as much as I did, swears that she can still hear that voice. Indeed, certain of his phrases, particularly those relating to hard and inclement weather, have become built into the family lexicon. A snowy or hoar-frosty day seldom passes without one of us saying in Kenzie-speak: "well it ain't what I'd call cold, Colin."

After the first edition of the book appeared, I interviewed Kenzie in the Anglia Television programme *Countryman*. Even in the unnatural confines of a studio he achieved what must still rank as a TV 'first'. I asked him to call some geese. The resulting sound, which had fooled hundreds of lost pinkfeet in its day, came very close to putting the station, sound-wise at least, off the air. The engineers just couldn't cope with the volume!

Sadly and unexpectedly for a man who had lived such an open-air life, Kenzie died at the age of 63. His charming wife Cicely followed him in April of this year.

Colin Willock,
Walton-on Thames,
June 1997

Preface to the Tideline Books edition

A number of Kenzie's friends and acquaintances have helped in the production of this new edition of Colin Willock's biography. Some have supplied the previously unpublished photographs, at least in book form, and without their help these simply would not have appeared. Those to whom I am most grateful are Bob Ashby of Oxford, Don Andrew of Spalding, Trevor and Mrs. Amos of the Gedney Drove End W.A., John Cooper of Norwich, Brent Pope of Blakeney, Mike Haig of York, Tony A. J. Van Clarke of Mablethorpe and Dennis Stephenson of County Down, and of course Colin Willock, the author. Others helped in smaller but no less important ways.

My acquaintance with Kenzie came about one frosty morning after flighting geese from Shep White's access. A friend Dennis and I were preparing to return home to the Midlands after a fruitless flight, when down the lane towards the Pill Box chugged a figure astride a Lambretta motor scooter. The fairings had been removed exposing the engine and the stocky figure astride it wore a Solway Zipper emblazoned across the back of which was the word KENZIE in large block letters. This was obviously intended to identify him to his clients when out on the saltings, as well as a blatant piece of self advertising. Kenzie introduced himself and we chatted for a while as fowlers, who meet after flight sometimes will, then we went our separate ways.

At that time I was the secretary of a Midlands wildfowling club and one of my jobs was to organise entertainment for the clubs monthly meetings. After a few enquiries I booked Kenzie to come to give a talk and show his wildfowling film at the clubs H.Q. in the Midlands. An unforgettable night ensued concluding with Kenzie doing some goose calls which nearly split the ceiling of the Cellar Bar.

Although the friend and I continued to flight the geese on the Lincolnshire saltings for several years, we never saw Kenzie again, but since I had asked him to autograph my copy of *Kenzie – The Wild-Goose Man* (and he had obliged with a small drawing of a flight of geese in biro above his signature) I was content.

In the same year, 1969, I had succeeded in shooting my first pinkfoot at 1:15 in the morning under a full moon from behind the sea-wall, when a party of geese were returning to the marshes from feeding on the fields. Every 'fowler's first goose should be set up as a reminder of the event and mine stares unblinkingly at me as I write.

Many tides have crept up the muddy creeks and slipped silently across the saltings of the Wash since that year and Kenzie at the age of 63 has long since joined the great majority. To prevent vandals dismantling his father's houseboat for souvenirs, Kenzie's son set fire to and burnt it much in the manner of a viking chieftain's funeral of which Kenzie would no doubt have approved.

If Kenzie's spirit lives anywhere it will be out on the gale-swept saltings of the Wash, but a large part of his exciting life is written here...

Geoff R Worrall
Tideline Publishing Co Ltd
July 1997

1

IT IS SUMMER now and the cars hum along the road between King's Lynn and Long Sutton. Their occupants hardly give the landscape a second look, some because it is too familiar, but many because they find it uninteresting, by which they mean flat.

The land here is flat, for it was until recent times owned by the sea. Apart from an occasional belt of trees and the spike of a church spire it has few vertical features. On the inland side of the main road, towards Wisbech, the landscape is bare enough, but between the road and the sea wall it takes on a fresh quality of loneliness. Single houses stand unexplained among huge chessboard fields. They look isolated in full summer, but in winter they will resemble a handful of child's bricks scattered about an empty playground.

Everything here is drawn in straight lines: the field boundaries, the dykes, even the rivers themselves as they run in artificial channels to the Wash. Ouse, Nene, Welland, they are part of the great drainage plan that reclaimed this land in the first place, and their outfalls are the only breaches this part of Lincolnshire allows itself in the defences it sets against the North Sea. The grass-covered sea wall, twenty feet high in most places, runs from King's Lynn to Boston and beyond. It is a sign that this land is on uneasy tenure and that the sea regards it jealously.

Just as the main road divides two sorts of countryside, so the sea wall is the frontier of a third world. Beyond it the change is a far more startling one. Once over the sea bank you are in the kind of outdoors that most urban men and many countrymen would find completely foreign. At first you stand amid emerald green vegetation, but the emerald is the green of the sea. The soil in which the sea asters and crab grass grow is soft to the feet and smells of iodine, for this is the sea's territory proper. As the line of driftwood shows, the highest tides flow all the way up to the bank.

Now it is low tide and the sea seems miles away, as indeed it is, whispering soundlessly far out on the sands—Breast Sand, Bulldog Sand, Thief Sand, Old South, Mare Tail, Blue Back, and Black Buoy. You can walk out down the marsh towards these sands but unless you know every feature of the place you will be unwise to do so. These are the great Wash saltings, and soon the tide will come hissing in with a hundred flanking and encircling movements. It is easy to get cut off even in summer when the marsh is almost friendly.

Walk down the saltings now with someone who can bring you safely back and you will notice the landscape change with the colours of an unfamiliar spectrum. The emerald soon gives way to a darker green as you reach the spiky grass which the marshmen call the stalk edges. Now brown is beginning to predominate, the brown of the fissuring capillary creeks that widen into arteries as they feel their way towards the open sea; the brown of the spartina grass—"spartini" to the local wildfowlers—clumps of which will swallow a wounded goose so that not even a labrador can find it. Then you are in a world of luminous elephant grey with not a sprig of vegetation, unless you count sea weeds. The creeks here are deep enough to hide a man, the sea wall lies a mile behind, and the place has a lunar loneliness. Ahead again lie the true sands where the great grey geese packs roost in winter.

You can thank your stars this is summer still and you have a good guide to lead you back across the creeks, where the cat tide is already creeping, until you stand secure on the sea wall again.

The land that the wall protects is worth looking at also. It is a brown land though now much of it is under growing corn. It is rich land and it grows potatoes like nowhere else in Britain. The fields are enormous and apparently featureless. But then you see that they are divided by drains, which hereabouts are called dykes, and that these dykes provide a network by which a man could, if he were so minded, get about the countryside practically unseen, and this has its significance.

Stand still on top of the wall and you will find that the land is by no means as deserted as it looks. A hare sticks her ears out of the edge of the corn. Two coveys of partridges are dusting at the corner of the dyke. A cock pheasant crows and another answers defiantly. This is all the summer growth allows you to see but, when the corn has been cut and the fields are bare in winter, these flat lands will reveal themselves as some of the most prolific game country in Britain.

A man comes riding along the top of the sea bank on a decrepit bicycle. He is red-faced, of medium height, in his early fifties, putting on a little weight, but the way he drives the old bike along suggests that he is pretty spry. He will have noticed you a long way off, for you are something strange in a landscape in which he knows every fence-post. He may give you "good day" but he'll still be wondering what you're doing here. Almost certainly he will dismiss you as part of the summer scene, the kind of thing the marsh has to suffer occasionally at this time of the year, although it is no place for trippers or picnickers. The man might have come from any of the marshland villages like Gedney Drove End, Lutton or Holbeach St Mark. He has the case-hardened look that continual exposure to a wind that blows unimpeded all the way from Poland stamps on the faces up here. But there is more to the look than that. These marshland people are the descendants of the men who once lived on islands in an inland sea that stretched nearly to Cambridge. The fact that the Dutch drained the fenland three hundred years ago has never entirely convinced them that they are connected by dry land or allegiance to the rest of England. Long ago they made their living by catching the fish and snaring and shooting the great clouds of wildfowl that came to the inland sea in winter. Some of them do still. The man on the bicycle, for instance. Nearly out of sight now, he turns his bike off the end of the sea wall towards Sutton Bridge.

His name is known to every policeman, wildfowler, gamekeeper and even naturalist around the borders of the Wash. The name is Mackenzie Thorpe.

The "Lincolnshire Poacher" was a traditional song long before Mackenzie Thorpe (he is usually called Kenzie) saw the light of day, or of shiny night for that matter. Yet he is probably the most famous poacher which that redoubtable shire has produced. If Kenzie's accomplishments stopped short at setting a snare or knocking a pheasant out of a tree on a dark night, then I wouldn't have been prompted to write about him. There have been plenty of books about poachers and quaint rural characters. Kenzie is something much more than either of those things. He is an original, and a man of extraordinary talents and near-talents. It is amazing that such a man can exist and flourish in a largely urbanized society. You cannot tell the story of Kenzie without recounting in detail the whole catalogue of his misdemeanours, and, inevitably, poaching becomes one of the main threads of his story. But this isn't to lose sight of the fact that he is also a first-class practical naturalist. He knows more about the ways of Wash wildfowl, and of wild geese in particular, than anyone living, and I include the director of the Wildfowl Trust, Peter Scott. Hardly a winter day or night passes when Kenzie is not down on the saltings or miles out on the sands after the ducks and geese, and he has been doing this for more than thirty years. From these expeditions, which must now number not far short of 15,000, he has built up an unequalled fund of wildlife knowledge. He knows things which few, if any, other men left in England know. That is why I call him original. I wanted to record as much of this knowledge and background as possible before such things finally disappear and there is no one left to remember them.

There are plenty of contradictions in Kenzie's character. Why, for example, should a man who so obviously admires wild geese kill so many of them? I don't think it will be profitable to look very deeply for motivation. If you do, you are missing the point. Kenzie is close in instincts to many of the creatures he hunts. Also, his livelihood is shooting and I do not believe he could have made his living in any other way. Motivation? Do not search for it in a hard or deprived childhood and in any other psychiatrist's pigeon-hole. You might as well ask the stoat why he catches rabbits or the goshawk why she pounces on a pheasant chick. Kenzie is a natural born predator, but he has this over the ferret and the hawk: he is aware, as are neither of those creatures, of the bite of the night wind, the smell of the marsh, the threat of the keeper's coming, and the fact that the goose he kills today was only one month ago in Spitsbergen. These are the things which have given a thrill and an edge to his exploits, both disreputable and legitimate.

Mackenzie Thorpe is fifty-three years old and he has lived in Sutton Bridge or Long Sutton all his life. Mackenzie is a peculiar name for a Lincolnshire man, which is perhaps why most people shorten it to Kenzie. Thorpe is not a Lincolnshire name, either. You will find it among gypsies and if you look closely you will see that in this instance the blood runs true, for Kenzie Thorpe's father was pure Romany and his Christian name was even more unusual: it was Mackenzay.

Mackenzay Thorpe came south from Yorkshire in the early nineteen hundreds to work on the Lincolnshire farmland and there met Kenzie's mother, a Sutton Bridge girl. Kenzie was born in 1908 and the marriage was, in his own words, "a forced case and none the worse for that".

The Thorpes must have been a formidable clan. Kenzie's grandfather, Ambrose, on his father's side, is remembered as "a hell of a great man", and his trade was mending pots and pans. His grandmother, Leviathan, would walk down a lane, spot a pheasant on its nest and whip bird and eggs up in her skirt before the hen could squeak. Then there was a team of uncles magnificently and most biblically named—Bendigo, Dolpherous, Esau, Mark, and plain Alf. There was also Uncle Emperor who was, ominously enough, as things turned out for Kenzie, a gamekeeper.

The countryside of Kenzie Thorpe's childhood was that now almost unimaginable pre-automobile rural world sometimes preserved in faded brown photographs on country pub walls. In these, moustachioed gents in curly-brimmed bowlers and solid-looking men wearing button-topped flat caps and leather gaiters are seen grouped around smart horse-drawn equipages, about to set out on some long-forgotten heyday.

But the circle in which Mackenzie Thorpe grew up wasn't that of the sepia-tinted photographs. The gents in the curly bowlers and cloth caps were the farmers and tradesmen. The Thorpes' strata was a good way below this yeoman bourgeoisie. In those days, Lincolnshire farmhands led a peasant existence.

Work was always uncertain and atrociously paid. Kenzie's father earned sixpence a thousand for dropping and treading potatoes. He could put in 10,000 in a day, and few could do better, but five shillings was all he got for it. In a long summer's day he could reap an acre and a bit with a sickle. He was paid thirty shillings per acre, which wasn't bad in those times, but the work was only seasonal. It wasn't surprising that, with his first child on the way, he took Kenzie's mother and ran away to Sheffield where he knew he could make a living in the steel works and brick kilns. But the dirt and din of that city was no place for a man who had spent his own childhood in a gypsy tinker's caravan. Before long he was back in the area of Long Sutton and Sutton Bridge, and that is where Kenzie Thorpe found his early diversions and companions.

That Lincolnshire village society before the 1914 War must have been a strange one. It was liberally peopled with eccentrics and drunks. The pubs were open from seven in the morning until twelve midnight. When the farm hands had money in their pockets their employers had to bribe them to leave the public bar and get the harvest in. Mild beer was a penny a pint and bitter only twopence. The marsh villages were full of flight-netters and punt-gunners who scratched a living in winter from shooting and snaring wildfowl. And, though only one man in fifty could afford a shotgun, few did not carry a bit of snare wire or a catapult. Small birds were netted for food and profit, and some such as Josh Cobley and his wife of Long Sutton even went so far as to catch sparrows in clap-nets and paint them yellow for sale as canaries to townie innocents. In the midst of all this minor wrong-doing the law was heroically represented by two constables—PC Sandal and PC Jabus Dixon. From a very early age Kenzie Thorpe fought a long, long feud with both of them, and this started while he was still at the village school.

Kenzie, the eldest Thorpe, was packed off to school at the age of five while his mother, whom he describes as a great tough woman, had a succession of children. There were his three sisters, Mabel, Leiler and Lana, who died; his brother Bob who now lives over at Tydd and weighs twenty-two stone; Donny who grew up to shoot occasionally and wasn't much good at it; Lewis, "not a gunner at heart, though he once shot a wild goose—just one". And Verdon who is now forty-one, never swore in his life, works hard, lives on his own, once did a bit of poaching but never took to it seriously, and who—and maybe it is by way of explanation of this abnormally virtuous life—"stands no bigger than six pen'north of coppers".

School left barely a mark on Kenzie beyond those regularly engraved on his bottom. Mr Everett, the school attendance officer, wore a path to the Thorpe front door. Kenzie remembers him as a big old man but he was no match for Mrs Thorpe, a big young woman, who was quite willing to belt the living daylights out of her own flesh and blood but was not prepared to see anyone else do it, at least on her own front door-step. One day Mr Everett arrived to make the usual complaint. Thorpe wasn't at school. Mrs Thorpe came to her son's rescue. "He's been helping me with the washing," she said.

"You send him straight along, then?" "I'll send him when he's had his dinner." "You send him right now."

"You've had your dinner, haven't you, Everett?" "Yes." "Well, I'll send him when he's had his."

But his mother's support was unpredictable. More often she lent it to the opposition, leading the punitive expedition herself and with considerable violence. There was always someone at the door complaining: "Kenzie done it." What Kenzie had actually done could cover a wide field. It included such things as being run in by PC Sandal for pelting telegraph wires with stones (he had actually been pelting sparrows). This summons resulted in the first of a long line of appearances in court and the smallest of a long series of fines: one shilling. The complainant could equally easily be the owner of a pear orchard into which Kenzie had driven some horses to rub down the fruit during the night. Or it might be Charlie Marsden, "a wonderful strong fellow with a stiff leg", whose strength and agility Kenzie had tested by pulling the axle-pin out of his potato-cart with a fork so that the wheel fell off and the spindle buried itself in the ground. Charlie had passed the test with honours. Not only had he managed to lift the cart back on to an even keel but he had had enough steam left at the end of it to turn up at the Thorpes' front door to report once again: "Kenzie done it."

Almost the only person in the village who didn't repeatedly feel that "Kenzie done it" was Miss Ethel Watson who kept the small greengrocery which Kenzie passed each day on his way to school-or rather on the days that he had decided not to play truant. His school friends would dare him to nick trifles such as apples and oranges, or to hide them where Miss Watson wouldn't find them.

Miss Watson was quite aware who the culprit was, and sometimes she would catch Kenzie and haul him into the shop.

Kenzie employed his favourite ruse. He turned on the "water tap". This didn't impress Miss Watson, who was too genuinely soft-hearted to be taken in by imitation distress. She charmed Kenzie. "All right," she would say, "I know you did it, but I also know the other boys who put you up to it, so you can stop pretending to cry."

Kenzie was so impressed with both her big-heartedness and her shrewdness that not only did he cease plaguing the life out of her, but voluntarily ran her errands. Today, now a very old lady, Miss Watson sometimes visits him and her refrain remains unaltered:

"It wasn't always you, Kenzie. The others put you up to it."

At the time, though, she was perhaps the only person in Sutton Bridge to take such a broadminded view.

Understandably, where her first-born was concerned, the imposing Mrs Thorpe got into the way of shooting first and asking questions afterwards. Once, when she caught him bathing stark naked in the Nene when he was supposed to be at home minding the kids, she opened up on him in the water with half bricks, but without scoring a hit. On another occasion her aim was more accurate. A neighbour had complained that Kenzie had perpetrated some hideous crime whose exact nature he cannot now recall.

"Mrs G's been telling me a rare yarn about you." "She's a liar," said Kenzie on principle.

Mackenzie Thorpe, who has hit more than his share of moving targets, recalls with some admiration that his mother "caught me square on the crazy bone with the dust-pan just as I was skidding out of the door". As a result he spent eighteen weeks in Lynn Hospital and today shoots left-handed.

One sort of crime Kenzie tried to hide from his parents. While he was at school, at least, he managed to keep his poaching activities pretty well to himself. For one thing he knew his father would disapprove—

at least of him being caught. But, more important, outwitting animals even in a small way was the breath of life to him. It must have been the influence of grandmother Leviathan at work. "When I was a kid I was just like a cat. I could have a hen-bird off her nest before she knew what was happening to her. I remember my father saying to me once: 'You've been after game all your life. When you could only crawl you got lost and we found you down a rabbit hole.' Well, he was right. I was never at home in the nesting season. And never at school neither. We used to have pigeon's-egg custard regular at home.

"I spent a good deal of my time hotching. Hotches are what gypsies call hedgehogs. When we caught them we used to rub them on their backs until they stuck their little noses out and then we'd knock 'em out with a stick. Once they were dead we bled them and put them over some flaming sticks which burned off the fur and spines. Then we'd take 'em off the fire and cut them down the middle, open them out, and wash them. The flesh looked beautiful. Dad'd roast them over a red fire. They're that fat it isn't long before they're talking to you. Taste? They're just like pork. That's how it was year after year until I come about ten."

Though Thorpe senior was quite up to cooking the bag he wasn't, it seems, much of a hand with a gun. Perhaps this was why he tried to keep his eldest away from fire-arms, though I think it is more likely that he could see trouble coming. "He couldn't," recalls Kenzie, "hardly shoot a hare setting in her form, though he did once say he'd knocked over eight sitting partridges with one shot. But I never knew the truth of it, for he only brought seven home and when he went back to fetch the eighth it had flown away. Or so he said. Anyway, I could see that he aimed to keep me off gunnin'" (the word is pronounced with a broad Midland "u" so that it is practically goonnin'). "But he'd lost before he'd started."

School continued without making any visible impression. "I never learnt to read or write properly, though I wish to hell I had, but I was top at everything athletic. Later on, I did the mile in 4.42, and it stood me in good stead many a time."

So it did, for collisions with PCs Sandal and Dixon were becoming more and more frequent. There was the time that Dixon caught Kenzie and Ernie Burton, who will appear in full force soon enough, up the trees at Curlew Lodge knocking down young rooks. When

Dixon had them cornered they dropped a sackful of rooks on him from the branches and ran for it while he lay winded on the ground.

At last Kenzie Thorpe and school parted company. Neither felt it could do anything further for the other. Kenzie apparently expected the mere act of leaving to perform a miracle for his stature and personality. The night that he left, a class-mate, Ted Crisps, tried to pick a fight with him. "You want to be careful, now," Kenzie warned him. "I've left school, you know." He was twelve years old.

In fact, leaving didn't change his personality. It simply confirmed it. Hotching and egg-collecting were child's play. He was a man now. Goonnin' was the thing.

The story of Kenzie Thorpe's obsession with guns and gunning between the ages of twelve and fourteen is a minor saga. It began on Fred Morris's farm where he went from school to work with another twelve-year-old, Ernie Burton.

Rashly, Mr Morris had given Kenzie the job of scaring rooks off the corn with an old muzzle-loader, but the muzzle-loader was too slow and cumbersome for what Kenzie had in mind. One day Ernie came to him and whispered that he had seen an old single-barrel knockabout gun in one of Mr Morris's sheds.

"Why don't you pinch the damn' thing?" Kenzie asked. Next day Ernie came round with the gun wrapped in a sack. He had a box of cartridges, too. The box was red and decorated with a hand that held a flash of lightning, and the price marked on it was "3s.". They took gun and cartridges to a field two miles from Fred Morris's land and tried her out. She went. They wrapped up the loot and slid it into a tunnel in a dyke. Then came the big moment. "Can't you get yourself a gun?" asked Ernie, who now felt superior and confident. "I seen one in Stan Brooks's buildings."

In the morning Kenzie was round there. He bid Mr Brooks good day and slipped into the shed. On a shelf was the gun, just as Ernie Burton had described it. He broke the gun and examined it. It was, Kenzie remembers, "as full of rust as hell's full of davils."

"Now then," he said to himself, "tonight I'm going to have you." He put the gun back and eased a slat off the window, then he nipped outside and wished Mr Morris good day again.

As soon as it was dark he squeezed through the window and

grabbed the gun. He ran a mile with it to Ernie's. "I gotta gun. She's a double." Ernie was favourably impressed. "Monday night," he told Kenzie, "we'll have a run out." Kenzie went home and hid the ancient twelve-bore in the top of his father's pig-sty.

That Monday night couldn't have been better for the purpose. It was pitch dark and blowing half a gale. They left home full of hope at seven o'clock and walked across Mr Morris's stubbles. Every now and then they blundered into a roosting pheasant or a jugged covey of partridges. Their knees were knocking and so were their hearts. A covey got up and they let drive with three barrels in the general direction. To two small boys the noise must have seemed appalling. Sick with anxiety they ran to the spot where they judged a pile of dead birds would be and found not a feather. Several more fusillades went the same way before they decided that they had made such a commotion that Sandal and Dixon must shortly come pedalling down on their tails with a column of reinforcements from King's Lynn. There was nothing in the bag and they were badly shaken, so badly in fact that next morning Kenzie sneaked the gun back. He told this to Ernie who had the wind up also. "Here," said Ernie, "you can keep mine."

But when PC Dixon hadn't turned up after a week, the thrill of those wings whirring without warning in the dark returned. Kenzie said to Ernie Burton: "Don't you think we ought to have a trip out? This time we'll do it different."

They went to the New Road by the Nene outfall. Now Kenzie was in charge. At a belt of trees close to the West Lighthouse Kenzie called a halt and pointed up into the bare branches. "Pheasants," he hissed. He put up the old single barrel. He fired and down came a bird from the night sky. It was a wood-pigeon.

By previous arrangement they were to have alternate shots.

Kenzie spotted two birds in the next copse and recognized their long-tailed silhouettes as belonging to magpies. Ernie had the gun and Kenzie wanted it back. "Shoot boy," he ordered. The disgusted Ernie collected a magpie. Kenzie seized the gun and led the way at a gallop to Rookery Bank and there he saw quite another sort of bird with a long tail roosting in the branches. Down it came, stone dead, a pheasant. "Here, you have the pigeon," invited Kenzie. "Thanks," said Ernie, who at this stage still felt he was being done a favour.

Fosdyke Wash

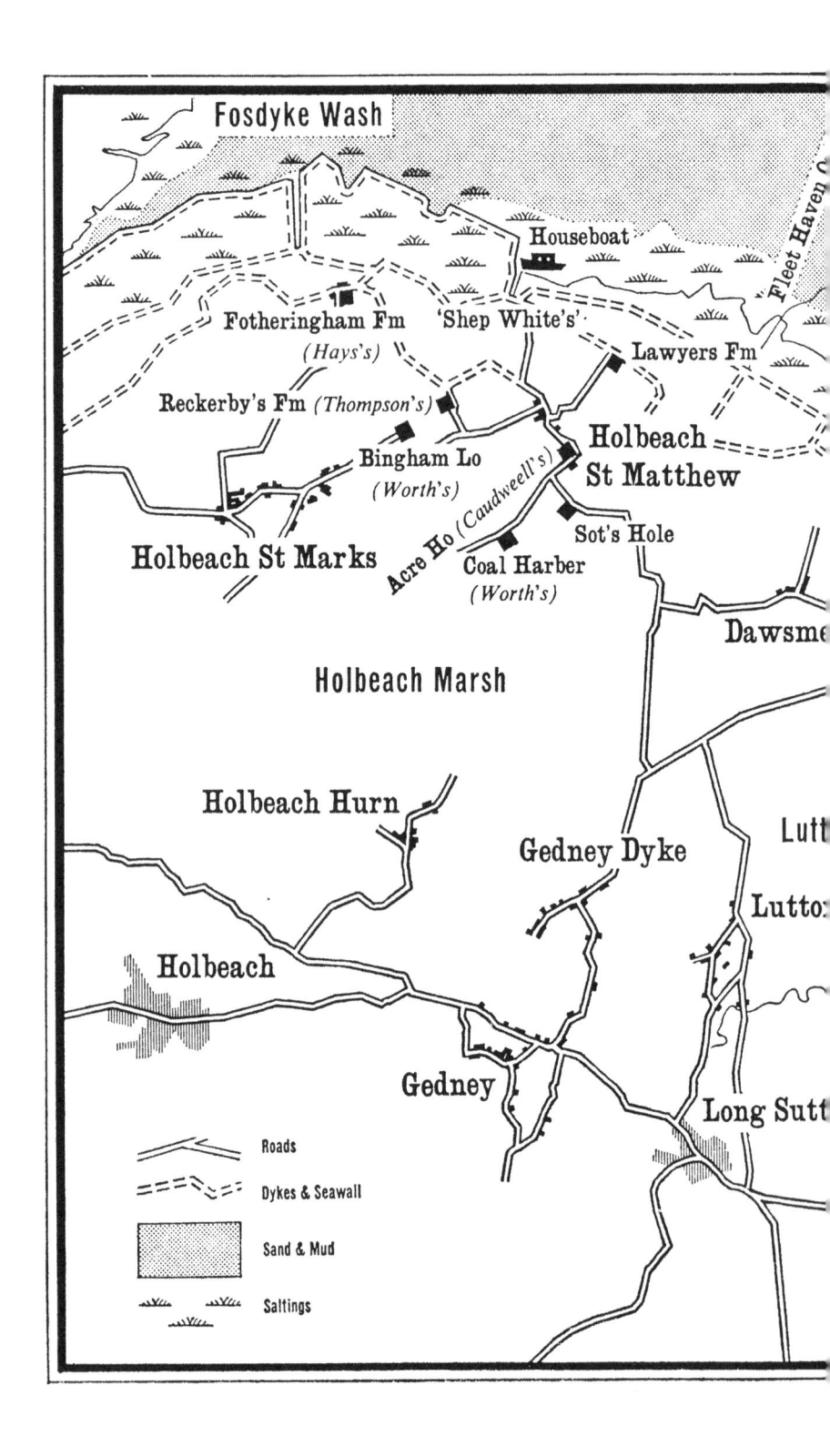

Houseboat

Fotheringham Fm
(Hays's)   'Shep White's'

Lawyers Fm

Reckerby's Fm *(Thompson's)*

Bingham Lo
(Worth's)

Holbeach
St Matthew

Acre Ho *(Caudweell's)*

Holbeach St Marks   Coal Harber   Sot's Hole
(Worth's)

Fleet Haven

Dawsme

Holbeach Marsh

Holbeach Hurn

Gedney Dyke

Lutt

Luttoi

Holbeach

Gedney

Long Sutt

— Roads
=== Dykes & Seawall
▒ Sand & Mud
⋎⋎ Saltings

The Wash

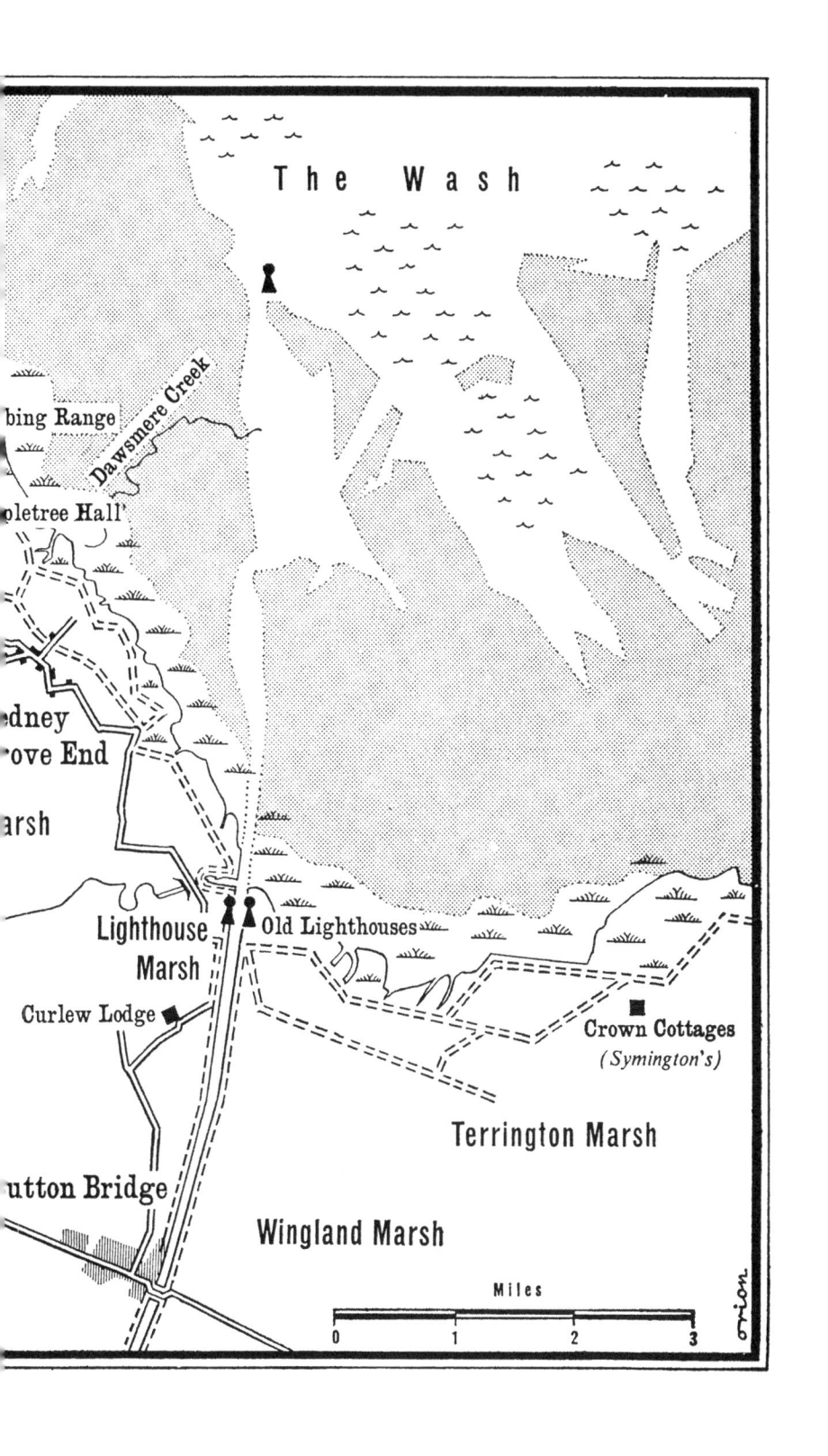

bing Range
Dawsmere Creek
pletree Hall
dney
ove End
arsh

Lighthouse
Marsh
Old Lighthouses
Curlew Lodge
Crown Cottages
(Symington's)

utton Bridge

Wingland Marsh

Terrington Marsh

Miles
0   1   2   3

orion

In some tall poplars Kenzie spotted a pair of crows. "Go on, Ernie, there's a pigeon to go with yourn." Ernie fired and collected a crow. "Gi'e us the gun back," ordered Kenzie. His next effort scored again with a pheasant which had been roosting on a low bough. They soon came upon another pheasant. Unavoidably it was Ernie's turn. Ernie took deliberate aim. "Don't you miss it," ordered Kenzie and poked him in the ribs, half hoping he would. But Ernie connected and a fine cock came crashing down nearly on his astonished head. He was even more astonished when Kenzie let him keep it, but, this was only because Kenzie's sharp eyes had registered danger. Two large dogs were sniffing towards the boys round opposite ends of a potato grave.

Kenzie seized the gun. "If those dogs get together on us I'm going to gi'e them one," he said, and drew back the hammer to show that he meant it. But the dogs, who belonged to the foreman, somehow never got together and the boys decided to run for it. A quarter of a mile away on a road called The Avenue they stopped to catch their breath. Up in a tree above their heads Kenzie saw a cock-bird. He leant against the tree to take good aim and learned a sharp lesson, for the recoil of the twelve-bore nearly hammered him into the trunk. The pheasant, crippled, flummoxed down and flew away over a low dyke. Kenzie plunged after it. A few minutes later he was back with the bird, but soaked through.

Back in Sutton Bridge, his father met him as he was unloading his three pheasants in the kitchen. "Wherever did you get those?" he asked.

"They was roosting in them young firs at King's Creek. I hit them on the head with a stick."

But when he came to eat his Sunday lunch Thorpe senior nearly broke a tooth on a shot. "That was a strange stick you were using," was all he said.

So Mr Morris's old single-barrel took over "he empty hiding place in the roof of the Thorpe pig-sty. It came out almost nightly and did fair execution. One night Kenzie, a small boy for his thirteen years, came home practically buried beneath eight dead hares.

"Wherever you bin getting them from?" asked his father, who must have had a fair notion of the truth if not of the answer.

"Lindsay Clark's been having a big shoot," said Kenzie. "The beaters got tired of carrying these big old hares and dropped them by the hedge. I couldn't see them go to waste."

Retribution may be a long time coming up in the Fens but it arrives eventually, as sure as winter. Two years after Ernie Burton had first produced the gun, Kenzie was plodding home along the dyke. He carried three hares he had shot after work that afternoon while hiding in one of his employer's ditches. He was then working for Lindsay Clark. He was nearly at Sutton Bridge when he saw a figure hurrying down the road in the dusk to meet him. Kenzie recognized the gait at a good two hundred yards.

"Is that you, boy?" his father called out. "Have you got Mr Morris's gun?"

"Me, Dad?"

"Yes, you."

"No, Dad. Not me."

"What's that you got in your hand?" "Hares"—the word is pronounced heers in those parts.

"I can see it's heers. But what did you shoot them with? Now look here, boy, Mr Morris knows you got that gun, and he's going to tell Sandal."

Kenzie wanted no part of the law. He extracted from his father the fact that negotiation was still possible. If the gun was returned no action would follow. But the gun was where he had left it—wrapped in an oiled sack and tucked in a dry drain. Kenzie went home and had his tea. Then he ran three miles to fetch the gun, and walked another four to Mr Morris's farm where he left the weapon propped against a big poplar tree by a hedge.

Kenzie Thorpe has the most extraordinarily photographic memory. Forty years later he can recall: "I laid it at ten degrees to the trunk. I daresn't put it back in the shed. That was Saturday night. Early on Sunday morning I borrowed my mother's bike and rode out to the farm, and there she was just as I'd left her, ten degrees to the big popple tree and a rime frost formed on the barrel. I never heard no more about it so I suppose Fred Morris must have found her. But I didn't have a gun no more."

Once possessed, a gun was something that Kenzie had to have again. He was fourteen now, and he had left Lindsay Clark's, possibly because of a noticeable drop in the hare population. He was working for another farmer, Copeland, and the first thing he did on joining was to search his out-houses for a twelve-bore. Copeland's produced him nothing. This was vexing because a grandiose scheme was troubling his mind. The size, scope, and daring of the project staggered him. He just knew that he had to try it, and to try it he had to have a gun. He borrowed his father's bicycle. In his free time he ranged the countryside on this, dropping into farms casually and searching the out-buildings. One afternoon he had a stroke of luck.

"I was riding down a bit of dirt roadway when I come across a caravan made out of a railway carriage. It belonged to an old fellow called Stan Phillips, who grew strawberries. He used the place to keep his fruit dry. I nipped in through the door and there was an old double-barrel that Phillips used to skeer the birds off his fruit. That night I was back for it. As usual, it was rotten with rust, but it was a hammerless, which wasn't too bad. I took it back to the dad's shed and dug a hole. I wrapped it in bags and buried it. Next day I bought myself a box of Remington's Cleanbore cartridges, in red cases, priced 2s. 6d. for twenty-five, and buried them along with the gun. I was all ready for off. Next Monday I'd set out as if for work, but I wouldn't go there. I'd go to Sandringham instead."

For a fourteen-year-old, poaching the King's coverts, for this was the plan, was a fairly big undertaking. It wasn't surprising, perhaps, that after cycling twenty-five miles with gun and cartridges the enterprise suddenly seemed too big, for when he arrived at Sandringham main gates he couldn't go through with it.

"It had got me beat. It was just too much for me. I could see myself in the Tower of London. But I wasn't going to give up. I rode on fourteen miles to Swaffham where I saw thousands of rabbits. I put the gun together and got ready to sort some out. Then I saw an old fox come running up the valley towards me. I thought: 'I'm going to gi'e you one.' But he never come in range, and then I saw why. There was a big line of beaters advancing. I was in the middle of a posh shoot. I thought: 'I've got to get out on it.' But when I jumped on the bike she had a puncture. So I began to run down a footpad, pushing the bike and hanging on to the gun, until I came to a wood. Then I dived in and sat down and mended the puncture.

"By mid-afternoon I was close to King's Lynn again. I saw a hare sitting by the road. I put up the gun but dursen't pull. I was that hungry that I stopped to eat my sandwiches practically where I'd started, by the Babingley River which runs through Sandringham. It was cold, and getting darkish. They'd been carting muck where I was sitting and I knew now I couldn't get home in time to pretend I'd been at work. I started to cry. Then suddenly I chucked the gun in the river and rode home as fast as I could. I never felt so lonely."

Three weeks later Kenzie left Copeland's and joined a company of threshers as water-boy. This was exciting, for threshers were a skilled elite and they had a certain air about them that appealed to Kenzie. What was more, they got around the countryside. One place they got to was Mr Mackman's down by the West Lighthouse. Kenzie inspected the out-houses as usual. Mackman had been drilling peas. In a shed was a new drilling machine. The container at one end held peas, but in a box at the other was a brand new double-twelve. Kenzie never blinked an eye when he spotted it, but at midnight he had the old dad's bike once more, and soon the old bike carried a familiar load—a shot-gun strapped to the crossbar.

There was wood fungus in the front room of the Thorpes' house in Withington Street and the hole it had eroded was just right as a hiding-place.

"For the next few weeks whenever Ma and Dad were out, at the pub or anything, I'd pull the old gun out and rub her bright with oil and sandpaper. How it happened I don't know, but my father found the gun, for when I came home from work one night they was sitting at the table not saying anything at first. Then my father said: 'Kenzie, you'm got a gun'."

I couldn't deny it this time.

'Well,' he said, 'either take it back or get rid on it'."

It was the second gun to go the same way. Kenzie threw it into the middle of the River Nene.

Mr Mackman's gun had been lying at the bottom of the river just three weeks when retribution arrived for the second time. It arrived round a corner of a Sutton Bridge street one morning as Kenzie was hurrying to work, and in the person of PC Jabus Dixon. The encounter left a marked impression.

"I can see him now. He was wheeling his bicycle as he always did with one hand held behind his back. Dixon stood straight up. He was six foot tall and very red in the face. He was a Scot or thereabouts a Scotsman. He grabbed hold on me and said: 'Now then, me lad.'

" 'Yes, sir!' 'I want you round at the station. Never you mind. You'll be all right.'

" He wheeled me off in double quick time. When we got there he led off straight away with: 'How long ago was you at Mr Mackman's?' I could see what was coming. 'Speak the truth,' he said. 'If you don't I'll lock you up. I think I'll lock you up anyway. Now have you got that gun?'

" 'What gun, sir?' I said.

" 'Mr Mackman's gun, my lad. Come on now. We'll find it all right, you can be sure.'

" I thought: 'Not without you can swim underwater, you won't.' I could see that he wasn't really certain I'd took it, and sure enough he wasn't. In the end he had to let me go, but that wasn't the finish on it.

" A year later I was off work, ill. I went round to George Hubbard what used to work with me and asked for a lend of his old hammer-gun to shoot rabbits. George gave it to me and I went down to a site where the Council were building some houses. As I was coming home with a couple of cartridges in the gun I met Dixon. Of course, I hadn't a licence, not that he knew that. He just thought I had Mr Mackman's gun.

" 'Got you, me lad. Got you, me lad. Got you, me lad.' He said it three times.

" 'Not yet, you ain't,' I said, and I climbed over the fence and cocked the old gun up. Dixon made to follow me.

" 'Don't you get over that fence,' I said, 'or I'll shoot you.'

" 'Don't you do that, me lad.'

" I ran off round the corner of the dyke and met Willie Fairey digging some potatoes. I hid the gun, still loaded, in a drain and gave Fairey sixpence to keep quiet. 'I'm running out the road of old Dixon,' I told him. I ran all the way to Long Sutton and jumped a lorry as far as Wisbech. Then I got another lift. I was going to run away to London, but at March I lost my nerve. I felt so lonely again. I set off back home.

" The dad met me at the door: 'What you been doing on?' he said. He sounded skeered. 'The police have been everywhere,' he said. I remember Mother was in bed with a confinement and he was worried it would upset her.

" I went to work next day just the same. On the way home who should I meet but Dixon. 'Now then, me lad, where's this gun?' "'It don't belong to me, it's Mr Hubbard's.'

" I could see he still believed it was old Mackman's.

" 'Never you mind about that, just you fetch it to me.' " 'When I've had my tea, I will.'

" It was November the fifth and very slushy. I took old Dixon round one and a half miles across the mud in the dark. He was slipping and sliding all over the place in his big boots. But when I came to the drain where I'd hid the gun he was close up behind me, and there was I trying to fiddle the breech open inside the drain-pipe so that I could get the cartridges out and save them. But the pipe was only eight inches wide and I couldn't get her open. He took the gun and the cartridges.

" 'Now then,' he said, extra red in the face, 'we'll see if it's Mr Hubbard's or not.'

" Well, of course, it was, and Hubbard identified it, but that wasn't the end on it. Three weeks later I got my second summons to appear in court. I was charged with threatening a policeman in the course of his duty and not having a licence. The dad came with me. I can remember Jabus Dixon standing there with his hands behind his back and saying: 'At twelve yards he held me up with a gun. He held it point blank at me.'

" All the magistrate asked me was: 'Would you have shot him, boy?'

" 'No, sir,' I said.

" They fined me three pounds and ten shillings costs."

Outside the court afterwards PC Dixon was heard recounting to a Long Sutton colleague how Kenzie had hidden the gun and escaped him. There was a hint of reluctant admiration in the phrase. "He's got runs like rats," Dixon said.

At sixteen, Kenzie Thorpe obtained his first gun, legally. It was a .410 and he paid £2 for it in instalments. Surprisingly, his father stood bond for this transaction, perhaps because he thought it would put an end to one evil, pinching, if not the other, poaching. Kenzie tried to reassure him by saying that he wanted it for duck, for he was now genuinely becoming interested in the possibilities of shooting wildfowl, which are, of course, anybody's game beyond the sea wall. But the

.410 was not man enough for the job, and soon he sold it cheaply to Ernie Burton, perhaps as recompense for Ernie's earlier "loan" of Mr Morris's single-barrel twelve. With the proceeds Kenzie paid the deposit on a single-twelve of his own.

One freezing night he was sitting by an inland flash of water waiting for flighting mallard. So far he had been singularly unsuccessful at outwitting wildfowl. He had heard, however, that decoys helped and that tame ducks often attracted wild ones. On this evening he had been at great pains to herd three Aylesbury ducks from a nearby farm into his flight pond. He had waited an hour in heavy frost for wild duck to arrive and all this time the Aylesburys had happily splashed and up-ended in the water. At last Kenzie caught a faint quack of approaching mallard on the night air. It was as if the white decoys had heard it too for they immediately waddled out of the water.

Kenzie was outraged.

"I thought: 'You old sods. After getting me freezing cold.' So I drawed back and knocked 'em all over with one barrel."

"Wherever did you get those?" his father said wearily when he got home.

An old schooner called *The Alert* used to put in to Sutton Bridge dock. She was in the coasting trade, carrying deal, coals, pig iron, almost anything to anywhere, so long as the destination was within the British Isles. She was manned by Danes and Kenzie had an acquaintance with many of her crew. He had even talked with the mate, Neilsen Hels, of signing on for a trip or two. He felt, in his own words, that "I wanted to get away from the village for a bit and clean my slate." PC Dixon and others felt the same way about things. (It had been a heavy disappointment for the law-abiders and law protectors when Kenzie's first attempt to break away had been blocked by an army doctor. The hand injury which his mother had inflicted with the flying dust-pan prevented him from taking the King's Shilling.) Thorpe senior had noticed *The Alert*, too. One night just before Christmas, 1925, Kenzie came home to find the schooner's skipper, Peter Mortenson, drinking *snaps* with his father. Kenzie went up to bed but left the door of his room open. By and by the Danish captain left, and Kenzie heard his father say to his mother: "Mortenson will sign him on. It'll do him a bit of good. It'll get him off this here goonnin' business."

"Ah," said Kenzie to himself upstairs, "you might think so," but he was pleased with the news just the same.

Next day he went aboard and signed. But *The Alert* couldn't get a cargo and lay there tied up for several days. Kenzie had a farewell gesture for Sutton Bridge. Penned close to the dock were three old gander turkeys and it was nearly Christmas.

The first night on board he sneaked ashore and whipped one into a sack so that no feathers should escape to tell the story of its disappearance. Then he wrung its neck and pitched it down the fo'c'sle. Next day they sailed. "We were still having turkey soup," recalls Kenzie, "after a week at sea, not that I felt much like it. First we took on mud ballast, then we unloaded it in Boston Deeps. By God, I was sick! We loaded coal in Boston, and we unloaded it at Dover, Falmouth, Penzance, and Newlyn. I was going to leave the ship there, things were that bad, only the skipper talked me out of it.

"We took on a cargo of china clay which we were to carry to Ireland. I remember the skipper had bought four oilskins. He'd got stuck with them and wanted us to buy them off him at a hell of a price. 'All right, you sons of bitches,' he said, 'you'll be glad to buy them in a day or two.' He was right. We hit a gale in the Irish Sea and lost a mizzen spar and had a man overboard. We nearly lost the schooner.

"On the very last trip I made with her we was running a wire rope in Bridgewater harbour, and I dropped a shackle overboard. Being a good swimmer, I jumped over and dived for it, but when I climbed back on the fo'c'sle the skipper hit me on the jaw for dropping it. We was never friendly again after that. I remember when I signed on that he told me, 'We tame lions here,' and he came damn' near to taming me.

"I quit when we got to the Manchester Ship Canal and bought a rail ticket for home. The porter said: 'You see those three fellers? Well, don't get in a carriage with them.' Me being daring dickie, I did just that. Two was rough looking and the third quite smart. I had my wages, naturally. They were playing cards, and the third chap, the smart one, who seemed a proper mug, kept winning. He was the kite, of course, not that I cottoned on, so when they asked me to join in I thought I'd win, too. They cleaned me out. I was skint. But I turned the trick on them. I started to cry. I could always turn it on when I wanted to. I must have damn' near broken their hearts—and they was made of flint—for they give me three quid back."

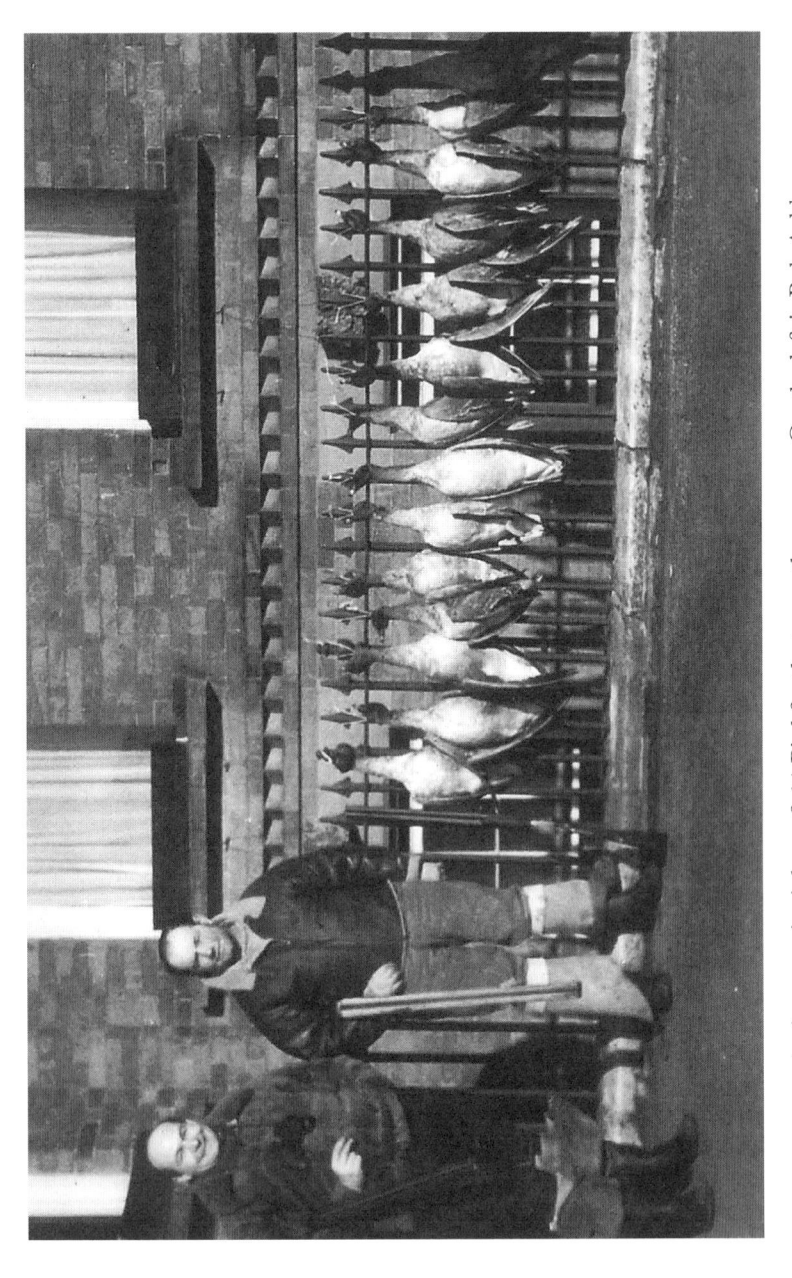

A nice morning's bag of 14 Pinkfeet between three guns. On the left is Bob Ashby, on the right, Kenzie. [Note the Double 8 Bore.] *Photo by courtesy of Bob Ashby.*

Kenzie returned to Sutton Bridge after only eleven months' voyaging. It had been hardly long enough to wipe all the marks off his slate. He arrived home on his eighteenth birthday.

The sea had taught Kenzie to use his fists. He had always been moderately handy with them. Now he decided to learn to use them properly. He bought himself a punch-ball and set it up on a tin roof outside his parents' house and drove them frantic by working out on it every morning before he went to the fields. Still, as his father reflected, boxing was more respectable than gunning and it might even earn the family a penny or two. This was important, for agricultural Lincolnshire had a thin time ahead of it. Before half a year was out Kenzie had turned pro, fighting as middle-weight at 11 stone 4, and usually for £1 a bout. Soon he was fighting twice a week, though still finding time to take the gun out at weekends. He was shortly to become middle-weight champion of Lincolnshire, and before he gave the game up he had won fifty-seven fights, eighteen of them with right hand knockouts to the jaw and one with a right hand k.o. to the solar plexus. He was eighteen and a half when he started boxing and twenty-three when he gave it up. Between those ages he met and married Mrs Thorpe. The courtship itself was not unremarkable.

The romance began as do many village love affairs. Two young men met two local girls on a spring evening in a Long Sutton street. Kenzie introduced himself as middle-weight champion of Lincolnshire and this undoubtedly made an impression. Often when girls wait in pairs to be courted by itinerant swains there is a distinct difference between them. One is usually far prettier than the other. Kenzie has no doubt that he got the better of this particular bargain, for at this distance he declares that his Cicely was "the prettiest girl in the marsh". They went for a walk. Kenzie took his girl to the cemetery, and there it was spring time, the only pretty ring time, and, if the birds did sing hey ding a ding a ding, it was doubtful if anybody present heard them. Kenzie says simply: "I fell in love with my wife that first night, and she liked me, and it's been like that ever since."

However, the future Mrs Thorpe's father did not like Kenzie; in fact, poor fellow, he liked very few people, not even himself, for he was given to the bottle. He drank so much beer that he was known as the

Nut Brown King. Moreover he was extremely jealous of his daughter.

Kenzie courted his sweetheart for six months before he discovered her true age. She had told him she was eighteen. She may well have looked it, for some parts of the country have a word for that kind of premature womanhood: they call it early ripe. In fact, she was fifteen. When he learnt this he said to his friend, ungallantly: "I'm going to pack her in." He didn't tell her that he had decided this. "I just ordinary left her."

But she had other ideas. She sent him a postcard imploring him to see her. Kenzie couldn't resist the invitation. He put on his best flannel suit and a pair of white gloves and bought an enormous box of chocolates out of his fight winnings. Then he cycled the six miles to visit her at her father's small-holding at Lutton Marsh. Her parents were out. "We made love, and came together, and we've been together ever since." The events that decided the coming together still lay ahead, however.

One Friday, when Cicely was in her early sixteens, Kenzie took her to watch him fight the middle-weight champion of Peterborough, Jim Simpkins. Kenzie was fouled in the eighth and passed out and his sweetheart fainted in sympathy. All in all it was a disastrous evening. Not only did both lovers end the fight unconscious, but Kenzie lost a big rose bowl. They trudged home in the pouring rain to Long Sutton. There a six-mile cycle ride still lay ahead to Cicely's home at Lutton. Kenzie asked his mother whether his sweetheart could stay the night, and Mrs Thorpe agreed.

Next morning, he took her back to her parents. The Nut Brown King was waiting. At first he didn't say a word. Kenzie began to walk out of the yard when the King came storming after him. "You want to git out of here. We don't want you in here at all."

Kenzie was prepared to go without a showdown, but Cicely's mother said: "Don't you go, boy."

"I'll go, I don't want no trouble."

Now the older man had picked up a double-handed axe. He came running up to Kenzie. "You'll get out of this yard in a minute. I'll cut you in half with this."

"I shouldn't do that if I were you, George," said Kenzie mildly. And then the axe came swinging at his head. Kenzie was in training, and this, after Jim Simpkins of the night before, was a sitting target. He dropped his future father-in-law with a right cross, sat on his chest, and "gave him some more to make sure".

Cicely was upstairs changing, but she had now come rushing down. Kenzie grabbed her like Sir Galahad and threw her across the saddle of the only available steed, his father's bicycle.

His opponent came running out of the house with a double-barrelled sixteen-bore and was putting it up to his shoulder when his wife grabbed at him and knocked him off aim. By now Kenzie and his Cicely were out of the gates and away round the turn in the lane.

"He was that jealous of his daughter, never letting her put powder or lipstick on her face, and always insisting that she be in by nine o'clock, and that full of hatred for me, that he'd have shot us both if his wife hadn't stopped him."

Cicely never went back to Lutton Marsh. She lived at the Thorpes' while Kenzie applied for permission to marry her. Naturally enough, the aggrieved father wouldn't give this, but Kenzie took the matter to court and, "seeing as how he was too ashamed to turn up, I won the day—and her".

They were married when Cicely was in her late sixteens. She was seventeen when a son, the first of six children, all now married, was born. He was called Mackenzay after Kenzie's father, and he turned out to be a very fair shot.

2

THE PINKFEET GEESE came to the Lincoln shore of the Wash after the First World War. Until the early 'twenties they'd been over at Wells-next-the-Sea in Norfolk. By 1926 they were being so heavily shot at that they decided to shift their ground. The movement was gradual, as you would expect with so cautious a bird. At first the geese sent small reconnaissance parties to Terrington and Wingland marshes on the King's Lynn side of the Nene outfall, and for a year or two these small parties would simply flight irregularly between there and Wells. Occasionally a straggler or even an odd skein wandered north-westward and crossed the Nene towards Sutton Bridge. Such a straggler gave Kenzie Thorpe his first goose.

It was the winter of 1924, during the period when Kenzie was first trying his hand, fairly unsuccessfully, at wildfowling. He had gone down to the lighthouse marsh, which lies on the Sutton Bridge side of the Nene close to the East Lighthouse. The Lighthouse isn't a lighthouse at all but a memorial to the men who built the artificial course of the Nene between its mouth and the inland fen port of Wisbech. It was the Lighthouse which later was to become the home of Peter Scott.

A single pinkfoot came gliding in in the half light and pitched a mile away in the stalk edges. Kenzie, remember, had had plenty of experience of dyke-crawling after pheasants and hares, but a tidal creek is something different. The bottom and sides of such a channel vary from hard shell and grit to marine ooze so soft that it will quickly swallow a man up to his thighs. Along this gutter he crept and crawled for an hour and a half. First he and then his gun became plastered with grey mud. When he finally surfaced he was only fifty yards from his bird. It jumped immediately and he knocked it over stone dead. It was not perhaps a very glorious shot, but it had bagged a wild goose, and what's more a first goose.

Kenzie panted back to the sea wall and strapped his gun to his bike. Then he threw the goose over his shoulder and rode home with it.

"Everyone I saw in which" (a peculiar and recurring conversational mannerism this "in which" of Kenzie's) "was a shooting man, I showed it to him."

"They told me: 'You want to throw that away. That ain't no good to eat.'

"Well, I've shot and ate many hundred of them since, and a goose well cooked is all right, let me tell you. But I wouldn't have cared if this one had been poison. It was my first goose, and it was a great thrill, and it tasted better than all the pheasants and heers I'd had put together."

In the 'twenties, for Kenzie, the Marsh and its neighbouring farmland were the scenes of glorious forays against pheasants and hares, with gamekeepers apparently ill-prepared for the battle and the police certainly not the alert force it had been when Sandal and Dixon had been on the job. Kenzie and his companions enjoyed a series of adventures in which the leading characters on both sides, for the law and agin' it, behaved in a manner which Surtees would have recognized immediately and which at times seems not far removed from the antics of Shakespeare's bumpkin clowns. Another quality emerges, too, and this is the leading players' contempt for personal comfort, injury and, occasionally, danger. This toughness, and sometimes callousness, is, I think, pure marshland.

Some of Kenzie's early companions have now gone, like poor Ernie Burton who was washed overboard while returning from Boston in the fishing boat he bought himself after the Second World War. Others, such as Bill Dewsbury, are as much a part of the Sutton Bridge landscape today as the East Lighthouse itself; in Dewsbury's case possibly more so, for he weighed eighteen stone at the peak of his poaching form, and that was in 1927 when he and Kenzie teamed up regularly.

At that time Kenzie was working at Sutton Bridge unloading timber from the deal boats that tied up at the pier. Work was not exactly regular and so there was plenty of time, and need, for gunning. Even in those days a hare fetched two bob.

One snowy January morning Kenzie and Dewsbury left Sutton Bridge to spend three days on the marsh in a derelict hut that had eight years previously housed the German POWs working on the sea wall. The luggage they carried on their bikes and in their packs consisted mainly of cartridges, sugar, tea, cocoa, and a blanket apiece. By the time they reached the sea wall the snow was piling on so thick that they had to dismount and push their bikes through the drifts.

The expedition provided some mixed experiences as well as some mixed shooting. On the second night the snow came down so fast that they couldn't get out of the hut for morning flight at the duck, and they were, in Kenzie's words, "starved with cold". Dismayed only at the thought of the shooting they might be missing, Kenzie proceeded to skin one of the hares shot the day before, break up part of the hut for firewood, and then, with the aid of snow that had drifted in under the door, make a stew in a frying-pan. With some nourishing hare broth inside him, he decided as soon as daylight came to attempt to wriggle out through a tiny ventilator in the roof—it was out of the question for Dewsbury to try—and then to dig the hut out. A good deal of the morning passed in these endeavours, but at last he could open the door and release the monumental Dewsbury.

"Whatever were you doing?" said Dewsbury, who was tucked up in both Kenzie's and his own blankets. "I thought you were never goin' to git here."

"Never you mind that. You git on them white clothes and we'll go out after some more of these old heers."

The next evening, fairly loaded down with pheasants and hares, as well as legitimately come-by ducks and geese, they were walking home towards the point at which they had hidden their bikes. There were still some cartridges left. "We was shooting everything that got up before us," Kenzie recalls, "when I spied an old redshank sitting in the soft bottom of a dyke. Bill wasn't much of a shot and I said to him: 'See if you can give that old redshank one. I bet you can't.'

" 'All right, boy,' said Bill, and he slid down the bank and let drive just as the redshank got up and flew off whining and shouting all over the marsh.

"I said: 'Well, you never hit that one, Bill.'

" 'Small wonder,' says he. 'Just you take a look at my gun.' "So I did, and sure enough he'd blowed the end right off it. " 'You must have stuck it in the mud, Bill,' I said.

" 'Do you think so? What shall I do with it?'

" 'Just you wait until you get home, then you take it to the blacksmith and have him hacksaw the end off it. You won't know the difference'— and no more he did."

A month later they were out together again. Kenzie always had, and still has, a master plan for every shooting operation. This time they were to borrow, though not necessarily with the owner's knowledge or permission, a flat-bottomed boat. In this they would drift down the Nene, tie up just short of the mouth and assault the hares, of which there were considerable numbers on young wheat in enclosed land just beyond the river embankment.

Kenzie started to call the hares from a dyke bottom. Calling hares was a piece of fieldcraft he had inherited from his gypsy forbears. Even today he does not know how or why it works, and even expert naturalists have admitted that they are baffled. The noise is a peculiar moaning sucking of the lips which rises in intensity and volume until it becomes almost hysterical. What the hares take it for passes understanding; it is like no noise that the creatures normally make in nature. In fact, the only noise a hare is heard to make is a high-pitched squeal, and then only when it is wounded. Perhaps the explanation is ultra-sonic. Possibly the sound touches something in the hare's hearing which is not detectable to the human ear. Whatever the explanation, the truth is that Kenzie's hare-calling works miraculously. Hares pop their ears out of the corn, listen, and come lolloping up as the rats did to the Pied Piper. Two came now. He knocked them over with a left and right but he didn't attempt to pick them, preferring, as always, to leave the gathering to the end of a shoot, or even until darkness, rather than attract attention. He called again and two more obligingly came, but as he was about to fire he spied a black object—and the enemy at a distance is always represented thus in Kenzie's rememberings of past battles—approaching at the double along the top of the bank. At first he thought it was Dewsbury, but then, in the half-light, he could see it was a woman. At two hundred yards he made it out as Miss Flossie Longlands, the lady from the big house, and she was showing a fair turn of speed.

"I flew out and grabbed the heers, then I ran up the bank.

I pretended to go to the east'ard and doubled back to the west'ard. I ran down one bank and then nipped back up the ditch at the bottom, and at last I threw her off. But when I got back to the boat, to my dismay, it had tipped over with the falling tide and sunk. It took me three-quarters of an hour to bail her out, and then I loaded the heers and the gun and rowed across the river so that Flossie couldn't get up with me, and walked two miles home. I only had two miles, but Bill, on his side, had six."

When they met next day Dewsbury was not particularly bitter at the desertion. "I had to laugh seeing old Flossie chase you all over the headland," he said.

"Did you have a bit of a walk, Bill?"

"I did, and I had eight old heers sitting on top of me." "You didn't?" said Kenzie admiringly.

"I did."

"Well, you did very well in that case."

About this time Kenzie was trying to persuade his younger brothers of the delights of the gunning life. He had two notable failures with brother Bob.

Four or five hundred geese, an unusually large pack for the period, were making the most of a thaw to gorge themselves on winter wheat. Kenzie had persuaded Bob to come on a stalk. They'd already done an hour's creeping and crawling when a low-flying aircraft put the geese up. Bob was all for calling it a day. "Come on," said Kenzie, "it's only a mile to where they pitched." But when they got to the new feeding-ground a farmhand disturbed the geese again and the pack went back to its previous location. "I dursn't ask him to come no more, but he offered of his own accord, for it was back the way we'd come and Bob wanted to get home. 'I hope we get a shot this time,' Bob said to me."

This time they got within range. Kenzie dropped two geese with each barrel, but his brother only winged his two and they were both strong runners. Kenzie picked his geese and then sat down to watch while his brother chased the wounded birds from one side of a hundred-acre field to the other.

"When he come back he were right out for the count. He was scarcely breathing. He rolled down the dyke and washed his boots in the water and I should think he was three stone lighter when the mud come off. When Bob had got his breath back he said to me, and the words he used was this: 'If I hadn't have got a goose I should have shot you, Kenzie.'

" 'Should you, Bob?' I said.

" 'I should have,' he said. 'I can't see why you want to go chasing these old geese all over Lincolnshire.'

"'Can't you?' I said. 'It's the sport, man. It's the sport.'"

Kenzie had another go to convert his brother, and this ended with an offer of violence from Kenzie's side, for Bob robbed him of what Kenzie reckoned would have been his record shot at duck. Around 4,000 mallard had been blown into the Lighthouse Marsh by a north-east gale and were feeding in the stalk edges. Kenzie had issued his orders carefully for a creek-crawling pincer-movement which was designed to put the thick of the birds over his, Kenzie's, head. After an hour of exhausting work, Bob, who now weighs twenty stone and even in those days wasn't a light-footed man, found himself to his surprise within shot of twenty unsuspecting duck. So, in the language of the district, he drawed back and give them one. His shot put the whole 4,000 up and away from Kenzie, who emerged from his creek and bellowed:

"What did you want to do that for?"

"Well, I got four," yelled Bob triumphantly.

"Four. *Four.* Four be boogered. I could have had forty. If I can only git against you. If I can git against you, I'll put this on your nose—my fist."

More than thirty years later the incident still troubles Kenzie.

"I should have done, too. And those were the very words I used."

Cousin Kenny was of different calibre. It was with Kenny that Kenzie used to moonlight flight the large pack of wigeon which at that time patronized the Lighthouse Marsh and are nowadays seen there no more. The wigeon would come in to gorge on the lush green grass at the top of the marsh, and the cousins decoyed them, using the first birds they shot placed belly-up on the grass, to bring in the others to feed. They made some big bags, and they kept it up through a very cold December and January.

During much of this flighting, the marsh was flooded by the tide, and Kenny wore ordinary leather boots. Kenzie, who normally hasn't much regard for personal comfort—or discomfort—his own or anyone else's—suggested to Kenny that he might get pneumonia if he didn't soon invest in a pair of short Wellingtons.

"I can't afford them," said Kenny. "You'll lay yourself up, boy."

"As long as the old goonn keeps going off," said Kenny, "I'm not much bothered about what happens inside me shoes."

The force of the argument convinced Kenzie, who never mentioned it again.

Even at this time Kenzie was getting a reputation as a wildfowler. Local lads with a taste for the gun used to ask him to take them goose shooting, but he was careful whom he selected. One he chose was young Freddie Warner. He'd known him in his

boxing days, and Freddie seemed to have the right stuff. One foggy morning he took him far out on to the sands and there they shot a goose, two curlew and two mallard. Back against the sea wall Kenzie heard geese feeding inland and laid his plans for a combined stalk. He had previously lectured his pupil on approaching geese in daylight on what he calls "the level of the land", i.e. with no cover. The only way of getting near them, he explained, was to crawl forward, flat on your belly, and using your elbows as front legs. In this he anticipated infantry training of the Second World War, but with one important difference. The infantryman was taught to carry his rifle across the front of his body, cradled in the crooks of his elbows.

The encircling movement began. They were both fairly well in position when there came a shot from Freddie Warner. The geese jumped and came streaming over Kenzie, who upped and knocked down one with each barrel and reloaded in time to get a third. He looked to see how his pupil had done, but Freddie was running towards him without his gun.

"What did you get?" Kenzie asked. At a distance he could see that Freddie looked white, but he put this down to the thrill of shooting a first goose.

When Freddie came up he said: "I've blew me thumb off."

The following conversation then took place:

"You haven't." "I have." "You never."

"I have. I've blew me thumb off."

"So you have. It do look a mess. You've blowed it off right down to the thick part, and by Jove, don't it look black? Have you got a handkerchief?"

Kenzie tied Freddie's wrist up tightly and sent him off to Mr Delamore's farm which was two miles away. "I want you to go there and ask him to take you up to the Bridge to the doctor's. I'll pick up the geese, and your gear, and your bike. And don't stop. Keep going."

"Get me gun, won't you?"

When Kenzie recovered Freddie's old hammer-gun he found that the hammer was cocked on the fired barrel, and down on the loaded chamber. He deduced correctly that Freddy had been dragging his gun behind him as he crawled, with both hammers down. He had caught one hammer on an obstruction and had cocked it just enough to let it fall and detonate a cartridge. Recoil had accounted for the fact that this hammer had re-cocked itself.

At the hospital they took the remains of Freddie's thumb off, and soon he was back goonnin'. It was the only gun accident Kenzie has had among his wildfowling parties and this is surprising for, as you will see in due course, they have included some very rum performers.

Inland of the sea wall at Terrington was a newly enclosed marsh that was so thick with thistles that you had to wear two pairs of trousers just to look at the place. It provided an ideal cover for pheasants, and the open fields beyond, which were part of the same private property, were brown with hares. This enclosure was the scene of a splendid series of verbal duels between Kenzie Thorpe and an ancient called John Watson, a pensioner poacher who, in his extreme old age, had been put on to guard the place.

"He was," recalls Kenzie, "a grand old man. He was eighty-eight when he died and he was as hard as nails. I remember one morning coming off the enclosure and there he was in his shirtsleeves pumping water for the horses. I was coming up the road that particular morning, gloves on, wearing thigh boots, two sweaters, 'Ballyhava' hat, and a wind-breaker."

Old Watson saw Kenzie and snorted: "Huh. Whatever you lapped up like that for?"

"Well, it's cold, John."

"Cold be boogered. It ain't cold. You want to be like I was years ago when I used to go out with the old poont-goonn. I've had three inches of ice on each finger. I never used to feel the cold. I can't understand you, Kenzie."

"Well, it ain't a warm morning, John."

"Well, it ain't cold neither. You don't know what it is to be cold. And another thing: you keep off this here enclosure."

Kenzie naturally didn't keep off and a few days later he was back again with a companion called Jim Ransome, whom Kenzie describes as "a proper pot-hunter". They had shot several hares and pheasants and were approaching a dyke preparatory to climbing it and going to work on the other side when a head popped over the top.

"It was John Watson with his old peak-cap and his white beard.

" 'Now then, Kenzie,' he said, 'I've got you this time red-handed.'

"'It don't make a lot of difference, John,' I said, 'if you have.' " 'Oh? We'll see about that. Look here, if you don't stop coming on this here enclosure after these old heers and the few pheasants what's here, somebody else will have my—job.'

" 'Well, somebody else'll git it then.'

"'Oh? And for why?'

" 'Because you was one of the biggest poachers round here. I can remember the time when you used to set fifty or sixty sneers along these old banks. What about that?'

" 'Well, them days is gone. And you'm got to stop coming.'

" 'Well, we shan't stop coming while you've got charge of it, so cheerio, old feller, cheerio.' "

The richness of the enclosure as a poaching ground was by now known to several of the local gunners, and, in Kenzie's view, the place was soon going to get overshot. He therefore decided to organize one all-out driving day, captained as punctiliously as any of the more orthodox shoots in the neighbourhood.

He posted his flankers and walking guns and started to comb the first hundred-acre bay. "We were shooting pretty strong," he remembers, "when to our surprise we saw there was another party out. Over the top of the bank come four people and old Watson. They made tracks after us and we kept ahead, but they just kept walking steadily after us until we came to a creek in which the water was about ten feet deep and sixteen yards wide. Watson used to go across this in an old gunnin' shout—an open punt—and he pulled hisself back and forth with a rope, like on an endless chain. I put the party in the boat and sent them across. Then I pulled the punt back for myself. I'd just got halfway across when old Watson comes up on the far bank and he shouts:

" 'We'll be after yer. We'll catch yer. Don't you worry about that, Kenzie.'

"'That's all right, John old feller. I'm not worried. You keep comin'.'

"So when I'd finished pulling myself over I just drawed back, put the old goonn up and blew the bottom out of the boat. That stopped him from coming across. They had to go back two mile round and while they was going round we was having another drive.

"And that's how it was in those days, poaching all over, going where I liked and doing what I liked. And the rougher the weather the better. That's how it was. We was chased, and I was chased, hundreds of times, but we was never caught, and I was never caught, not until we got on into the nineteen-forties. But that was the cream of it, round about 1928."

Nineteen twenty-eight was the year in which Kenzie Thorpe turned professional wildfowler and started guiding visiting gunners across the marshes. It was also the year in which he met Peter Scott.

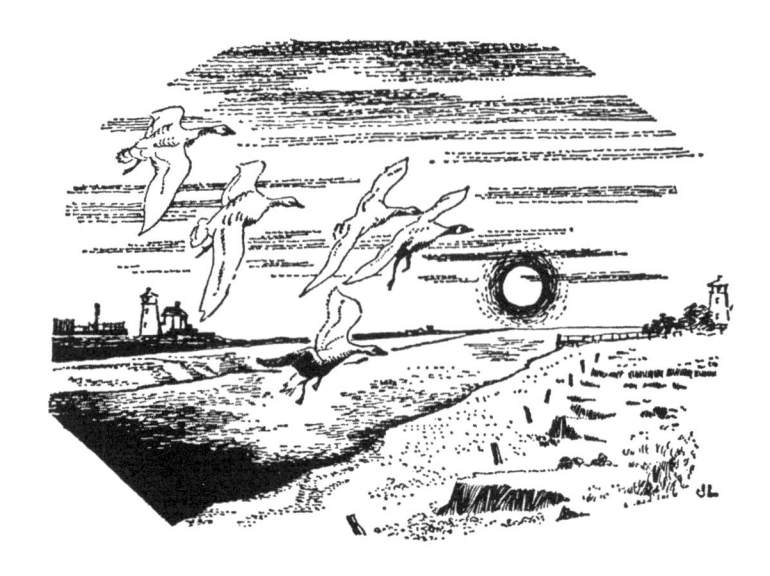

3

Most people today think of Peter Scott as a leading protector of wildfowl, and of wild geese in particular: and rightly so. I suppose a great many of the viewers who see him on television assume that he frowns on goose-shooting and goose-shooters. Anyone who has read *Morning Flight* will realize that the Director of the Severn Wildfowl Trust takes no such narrow view, for *Morning Flight*, Scott's personal wildfowling testament, is mainly about shooting ducks and geese on the Wash with shoulder and punt-gun, and often in large numbers. In his autobiography Scott tells how he eventually decided that he had shot enough geese, and of the incident concerning a crippled goose which made him hang up his wildfowling gun for good and all. Since he underwent this conversion—a change of heart liable to overtake wildfowlers who are, in the main, as much naturalists as sportsmen— Scott has helped frame legislation that gives a fair crack of the whip both to the man with a gun and to his quarry. The Protection of Birds Act, 1954, is the most notable example. But in 1928, when Peter Scott was still up at Cambridge, his mind was almost entirely on shooting geese: lots of geese. This was the year in which Scott's and Mackenzie Thorpe's footprints first crossed in the mud of the marsh. They kept crossing for the next eleven years.

Early one morning Kenzie was sneaking down an inland dyke on Symington's farm, Terrington Marsh. He was moving like an old fox, for he was after some of Mr Symington's hares. It was still dark, yet on top of the bank he spied the familiar black objects that meant opposition or at least interference. Like an old fox, he froze. He couldn't make out who the objects were, although he could see that they were swinging their arms to keep warm and this suggested that they were wildfowlers rather than members of a gamekeeper's posse. He approached very slowly because he still couldn't identify them. When he came up to them, one of the black objects—it was, in fact, Peter Scott—called out "Good morning".

"Morning," grunted Kenzie cautiously. "What are you doing here?" asked Scott.

"I've got permission to come here. Why?"

"I don't think you have. We're the only ones who have got permission to come here. What are you after?"

"Wild geese," lied Kenzie.

"Well, so are we, and we've been waiting here nearly all night for them."

Kenzie thought: "More fool you!" Anyone could see that the geese wouldn't come off the marsh until it got light and there was no moon to change their minds for them. Poaching hares was now out of the question, so he said: "I'll go in the opposite dyke. I shan't disturb you there," and walked off before the young gentlemen from Cambridge could argue. As he climbed the dyke he saw that they were by no means ignorant of goose-shooting for there were some dead birds set up as decoys in a potato field.

When it broke daylight the geese started to come in to the decoys.

Kenzie remembers the scene vividly. "Up used to go the barrage, sometimes eight or ten shots, and maybe a goose or two would drop out. The remainder used to fly over me too high to get a shot, though I was feeling so fed up that occasionally I had a go. At last one goose came very, very low past me and I give it two barrels and down it went on the field. I got out of the dyke and ran after the bird which was a

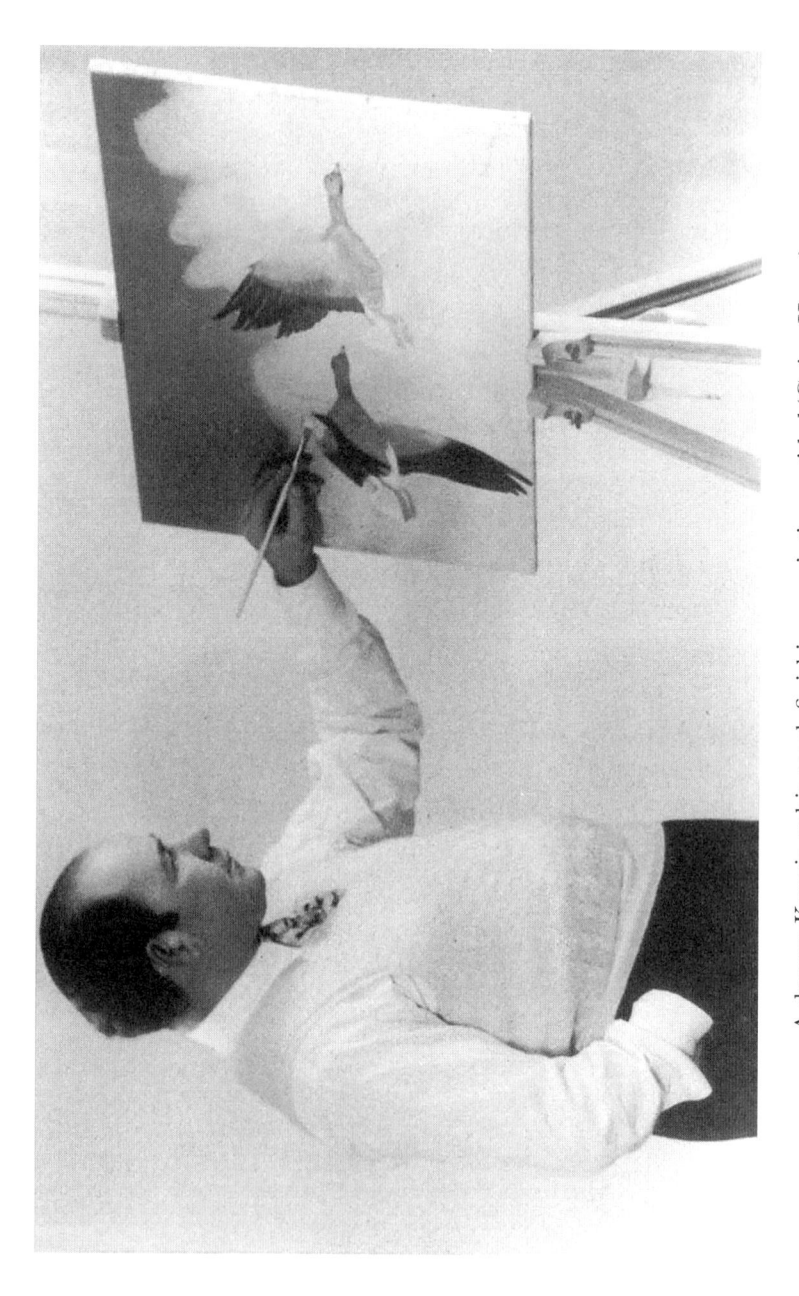

A dapper Kenzie at his easel, finishing a painting entitled 'Going Home'.
Photo by courtesy of Bob Ashby.

strong runner and caught it and wrung its neck. But when I looked at back of me there was someone chasing after me. I'd stuffed the bird inside my poacher's pocket when this young feller [it was David Haig-Thomas] caught up with me and let off with: 'Have you picked up a goose?'

"I said: 'Yes. Why?'

" 'I want that goose,' he says.

" 'Well,' I says, 'you can't have it.'

"'Oh?' he says. 'Well we'll see about that.'

"So he went back and fetched the other three guns, and Peter Scott was one of them, and Scott then had a go. 'Now then, old boy,' he says, 'just you hand over that goose.'

" 'Not likely,' I says. 'I'm sticking to that. I runned after that goose, and I give it two barrels. And you can try and git it if you like.' "

The squat business-like figure of Kenzie Thorpe with twelve-bore at the ready must have seemed fairly menacing in the half light of a Lincolnshire dawn, even though the odds were four to one. Or perhaps it was merely that a sense of fair play prevailed.

"Any road," says Kenzie, "after a few moments they drawed off, and I kept my goose all right."

About this time another well-known character, who has also subsequently had a good deal to do with both shooting and preserving wildfowl, arrived on the marsh. Kenzie had decided to capitalize on his growing store of wildfowl knowledge by taking visiting guns out to shoot ducks and geese. In his new role of professional guide, he had taken on a party of three undergraduates from Cambridge, "real wild, hard cases, who didn't care where they went and what they done".

That night it was blowing a seventy-mile-an-hour gale from the west. Kenzie led his guns out in a floundering, flubbering darkness in which the wildfowlers could hardly stand for the gale. He took them far out on the sands and stationed them in a deep creek. They stood there, having the breath blown out of them, for three long cold hours, waiting for the geese to come off the sands and flight inland to feed under the moon. The geese, however, thought that it was far too rough for night-flying and decided to stay put. Eventually, shortly after midnight, Kenzie marshalled his three hard cases and made a strategic withdrawal to the sea bank. A most unusual "black object" was standing close to the Cambridge men's car. It was well over six feet tall, sported a long bushy beard, was wrapped in every imaginable form of warm clothing, the whole considerable human edifice being crowned with a little beret. The figure was busy piercing a tin of pineapple chunks with his pocket-knife, drinking the syrup and then throwing tin and pineapple away. He disposed of three tins in this fashion while he told Kenzie just what was what.

"The geese won't come off tonight," he boomed. "We might as well go home." He said this with great authority, despite the fact, which was later revealed, that until then he had never shot a pinkfoot. It was, however, an opinion with which Kenzie entirely agreed.

"All right," Kenzie said, "and though I don't think the geese will budge in the morning unless the wind alters, we'll come back before dawn and try again."

"Right," said the stranger, "I'll join you. How d'ye do? My name is James Robertson Justice."

Next morning the wind had dropped a little and shifted a point or two. The party, reinforced by Justice, went out in the darkness to the creek they had manned the previous night, and the geese jumped and came inland, skein by skein, as they often will in rough weather. There were eight geese shot and Justice bagged his first pinkfoot.

Jimmy Justice became a frequent member of Kenzie's parties. He would roar in to Sutton Bridge in a large, noisy and ancient car and bellow to Kenzie almost before he had turned the corner of the street: "What ho, you old bastard!"—in the friendliest possible way, of course. In the end, Justice turned out to be a better punt- than shoulder-gunner, but this is jumping ahead several years. But for the record, his best punt-shot at wigeon on the Wash was seventy-five, made up towards Fosdyke.

Shortly after the pineapple incident Justice again booked a trip out with Kenzie after the geese. The third member of the party was a visiting gunner from Kent called Kenneth Bromley, who, Kenzie says, is one of the best amateur wildfowlers he has ever met. At this stage Bromley was a beginner.

It was a foggy, heavy rime-frost morning when everything on the marsh was "double thickness". The reeds were bent double under the weight of frost, and the spartina grass was flattened by it. As the three men plodded out the mile across the sands, known locally as "Poppletree Hall", their clothes, their guns, and even their eyebrows became coated with a layer of hoar frost. Dawn was still a long way off when they hid themselves in a creek to wait for the geese.

"Do you think they'll come off, old boy?" Justice wanted to know.

"They'll come off all right, sir," Kenzie told him. "You can hear 'em talking now, like they do just before they jump."

But as dawn was breaking and everything seemed set for an excellent flight, Kenzie once again spotted the approach, from the direction of the sea wall, of yet another group of black objects. Three of them appeared out of the fog. This time there could be no question of transgression for Kenzie's party were on the salt marsh, between the tide marks, where shooting is free to any man who knows how to get it.

As the three men came closer, Kenzie saw that it was Scott again with two of his friends. Scott asked the name of the sands and Kenzie told him. He also told him that there were two or three thousand geese out ahead of them.

"Good," said Scott, "I'll go and put them up. I love to hear the noise they make when they flight."

Kenzie, though aware of the charm of this sound, was more concerned for his shooters.

"I shouldn't do that if I were you, sir. I should let them jump. Let them jump on their own. If you push 'em all up in one crowd we'll hardly get no shooting at all."

"Oh, that's all right. I love to hear them. I'll go and disturb them."

"In that case," said Kenzie, "I can't do nothing about it. You'd better go."

Kenzie recalls: "We got just two shots as the result of Peter Scott putting them up, and Justice and Bromley weren't very pleased. But Scott had obviously made an impression on Justice for, soon after we come off that morning, Justice went down to see Scott at the East Lighthouse at the end of the Nene, which he was just then making his home. And very soon he had struck up quite a friendship. Justice amused Scott with his little jokes and that."

Kenzie in his own way had registered with Scott, too. Soon after Scott had settled in at the East Lighthouse he began to experiment with keeping wild marsh birds, and Kenzie used to go down in the shooting off-season to help him.

Peter Scott's first attempt was with waders, that edgy, cautious, hysterical group of birds, many members of which are found below the high-tide mark. Not surprisingly the experiment was a failure. Waders need the untrammelled freedom of the mud creeks and the tide-line. They do not take kindly to a pen.

Scott built his pen just below the Lighthouse and on the salt marsh proper. In it he tried keeping oyster-catcher, redshank, green plover, golden plover, curlew, knot and stint. The birds wouldn't settle down. They simply walked round and round the wire until they got too tired to walk any more. Then they packed up and died. After weeks of heartbreaking work, Scott admitted defeat. Waders demanded freedom and the survivors were given it. His mind turned to geese, and he commissioned the flight-netters of Gedney Drove End to catch him some.

Ironically, the 1954 Protection of Birds Act, on which Peter Scott had some influence, was to outlaw flight-netting, but the netters could have had no premonition concerning their client. Even had Scott been able to tell them what his future part would be it is doubtful whether the Drove Enders would have taken any notice. In Drove End they don't reckon much of London as a centre of the legal and governmental power. They demonstrated this in a historic lawsuit concerning right of access to a certain part of the salt marsh. When this case reached the Law Courts or, a point of appeal, Gedney took a village vote as to whether they should send representatives or not. The vote went against attendance, and as a result Gedney Drove End lost its case. It is no accident that one channel up above the Fleet Haven outfall is today known scathingly as Lawyer's Creek.

The flight-netters caught Scott his geese by a method which must be nearly as old as the snare of the fowler mentioned in the Bible. It consisted of stretching up to forty yards of home-made four-inch mesh netting between ash-poles across the green of the marsh. The siting of the nets was crucial. First, they had to be placed across natural flight lines. Then, due allowance had to be made for the effect of the wind on the flighting fowl. Lastly the nets had to be rigged so that at full tide the water would just clip the bottom edge. In this way the flight-netters caught trips of golden and grey plover, redshank, knot, curlew, parties of mallard, wigeon, teal, pinkfeet geese and occasionally brent geese as well.

Kenzie employed his own netting method, though he favoured a device sprung with poles and ropes that clapped over on roosting geese like a linnet net, and this required great fieldcraft, for, whereas the flight-netters went home leaving the tide to do their driving for them, Kenzie waited, hidden, to pull the string himself. He had some success, and his birds, together with those produced by the Drove Enders, found their way into the enlarged pen that Peter Scott had prepared for his first wildfowl collection.

Scott soon began to need some help with his birds. At the time he only had help of a sort, and this consisted of another notable local character called Samphire Charlie. Kenzie remembers him as a "big broad old man, proper Norfolk. When you used to talk to Charlie, all that Charlie could talk about was his old pin-fire goonn and his little dog, Peggy. With that pin-fire goonn he'd killed as much stuff––to hear him talk––as would take four horses and wagons to cart it away."

Charlie lived in a cellar below the cosy five-roomed Lighthouse.

He'd been there before Scott took it over as a wildfowling centre, residence, and studio, and he might have been able to stay there for as long as he liked after Scott moved in. Alas, he had no interest in the miniature Wildfowl Trust that was growing up outside. Charlie's means of livelihood were clamming, winkling, musseling, and, in the summer, gathering samphire grass off the marsh which he sold locally for salad. His leisure interest was beer.

"He could," Kenzie recalls, "tell a right tale. He was ver', ver' amusing. But he didn't amuse Peter Scott, who could never understand why Charlie wanted to bike four miles up to the village with his dog in the basket on the handlebars on his old errand boy's bike, to get a bellyful of beer. Charlie was a proper boozer, and Scott didn't like that, and after several years, sure enough, Charlie got finished."

Kenzie was still working on the deal boats while Charlie alternately boozed and samphired, but he went down more and more frequently to assist with the birds. He helped Scott to enlarge the pen and pinion the captured geese. He fed the birds and ordered the corn for them. Sometimes Scott would go away for five weeks at a time, leaving Kenzie in charge of the wildfowl, and also of Samphire Charlie. There was always a risk that unscrupulous local lads would come down to the marsh and blaze away at the geese in the pens, and, to tell the truth, there was nothing in law to stop them, for the goose pens were built on the public saltings. However, Kenzie knew from deep personal experience, how to deal with that sort of character. After all, hadn't he drawn back and given those three old Aylesbury ducks one. The best gamekeeper is often the ex-poacher, only Kenzie wasn't by any means what you would call ex-, Gradually he became, though still part-time, general factotum at the Lighthouse.

At the end of 1935 Scott's wildfowl collection was still quite modest, consisting of nine pink-footed geese and three mallard, but by April of the next year it had increased to: fifteen pinkfeet, three brent geese, one greylag goose, fifteen mallard, thirteen wigeon, two pintail, two shelduck, and one bean goose. The bean goose, one of the prizes of the collection, was caught by Kenzie, and in his own particular style.

Kenzie had spotted these nine bean geese feeding regularly on the short grass of Terrington salt marsh. He set his net, which he describes as a fly-over type, fifteen yards long by seven deep, where he hoped the party would feed, and hid himself in a creek. Sure enough, after several hours' wait, the geese came in and pitched within fifteen yards of the net. They walked upwind towards it. Kenzie pulled the cord and trapped eight out of nine geese in the net. But before he could pull himself out of the mud and water of the creek and get his numbed hands to work, seven had escaped. Kenzie did not recognize the remaining goose for what it was: to him it was just another, though smaller, grey goose. He put the bean goose in a rucksack, folded his net and walked four miles with it back to the Lighthouse. Peter Scott was away and Charlie wasn't particularly helpful when it came to identifying the catch.

"Cor," said Charlie, "I never seed one like that afore. You better leave it 'ere until 'e comes back."

When Peter Scott returned he sent for Kenzie and told him he'd caught a bean goose, a rare visitor to the Wash and a bird which sometimes mixes with white-fronts. Scott offered him a pound for it, and Kenzie gladly accepted.

By 1936 the Lighthouse collection had become a private Wildfowl Trust and its maintenance was getting well beyond the inclinations or capabilities of Samphire Charlie. So Charlie "got finished", and

Kenzie Thorpe was taken on by Scott as full-time assistant. Every day now he cycled down from Sutton Bridge to take up his duties.

For a man of Kenzie's tastes and even latent talents they were exciting duties. The point is a hard one to make to the rabidly anti-shooting faction, but it is nevertheless true: Kenzie, the implacable goose-shooter, was fascinated by, and felt strong affection and admiration for, wildfowl. Scott, who at that time was certainly killing his share, knew and understood this. To both of them, keeping and shooting wildfowl simultaneously was no paradox. It was all part of the same thing. Though this is no place for propaganda, this bond between hunter and quarry is a factor of which the anti-blood sports faction entirely loses sight. The bond is certainly more important to the survival of wildlife than all the well-meaning sentimentalism of the town-bred abolitionist. It is an odd possibility that if the hunters ever go, the hunted stand a good chance of going soon after. For the hunters are in the main the people who care about wildlife in the countryside and understand its problems, even though they take a reasonable harvest from it.

There was quite a bit that Kenzie could teach Scott about geese on the Wash and about marshcraft. And the relationship certainly opened up several new worlds for Kenzie. For instance, he discovered in the most practicable way possible what happened to the grey geese between April and October when they weren't playing hide and seek with him on the fields and saltings of Lincolnshire. A ringed goose nicknamed by Scott "Annabel" vividly demonstrated the pinkfoot's comings and goings.

Annabel, attracted by the captive geese, flew into the Lighthouse, a fully-winged wild bird, in September 1936. She took off for Iceland on May 15, 1937, but was back on October 9, 1937. She flew north on May 7 next year and when she returned in November 1939 she brought five wild geese with her.

There was plenty to lure Annabel to the Lighthouse. Shortly after Kenzie signed on full-time with Scott, the collection increased considerably. By 1937 there were 161 birds in the pens, including red-breasted geese, snow, blue snow, Ross's snow, Emperor, bar-headed, and Magellan's geese, as well as eight species of duck.

At this time Scott was painting almost continuously. Kenzie watched him at work on the wildfowl pictures that illustrated *Morning*

Flight and Wild Chorus and, typically, thought this was something at which he ought to have a shot, too. So, when Scott made one of his trips abroad to study wildfowl, Kenzie borrowed canvas, paints, easel and brushes and had a go. Surprisingly, the results, though on the crude side, showed promise. Kenzie never told his boss what he was up to, so he never received any active tuition or encouragement. Nevertheless, Kenzie laid the foundations of a modest talent, and today regularly sells his oil-paintings to wildfowling clients. It would be losing the place in his story to describe these in detail, but it is fair to say that they are by no means bad. When they are self-conscious they err on the side of the sentimental in treatment. When they are spontaneous they have a primitive quality that is most appealing. They certainly smell of the marsh as much as they do of paint.

The officially recognized part of Kenzie's painting duty at the Lighthouse was more prosaic. It consisted of painting uprights of the wildfowl pens the delicate shade of green which Scott's artist's eye demanded. Kenzie brought to his work the robust, outrageous, and sometimes callous sense of fun that is part of marsh village tradition. This often got him into trouble with Scott who was, one feels, a rather serious-minded young man. One such tiff concerned the green paint.

Kenzie was sometimes allowed to mix the yellow and blue that produced this special shade of green. He was doing this one day when the broody hen he kept for rearing young birds came fussing up to him. Kenzie regarded the exotic wildfowl all around him and decided that the hen could do with some decoration. So he painted her right leg yellow, her left leg blue and her comb green. Soon after he'd sent her indignantly clucking away and forgotten about the whole thing, Peter Scott came out of the Lighthouse with John Winter, with whom he'd won the international fourteen-foot dinghy event at Hunstanton. Scott had a bucket of corn so, of course, the birds came round immediately—led by the hen. Scott was angry.

"Did you do that, Kenzie?" "No, sir. Not me, sir."

"Well, I don't like that at all, Kenzie. I call that cruel." Kenzie was unrepentant. Next day, Ernie, the bullockman, came down to the Lighthouse to visit his charges grazing far out on the marsh. He left his bicycle propped against one of the pens. This was a mistake. While he was away Kenzie painted everything on it except the saddle green, and it seems odd that he should have stopped there. It was dark when Ernie returned, and so he didn't discover that his bicycle had changed colour, or at least to what colour it had changed. Ernie being a Lincolnshire rustic was not put out. Nor, when he met Kenzie the next day, was he going to give any points away. It was Bill Dewsbury with his six-mile walk home all over again.

"You did a right smart job on my old bike, Kenzie," he said. "That would have cost me ten bob up at the Bridge."

"That's all right, Ernie," said Kenzie, magnanimously. No further word passed.

There were other tiffs between employer and employed, which were, seeing the different backgrounds and similar ages of the two men, perhaps inevitable. Not unnaturally, Peter Scott liked to feel that he had everything under control and shipshape when friends from London or Cambridge called. He therefore suggested to Kenzie that he should buy him brown overalls for working in.

"What do I want those for, sir?"

"Just to smarten things up, Kenzie."

"I suppose I could come down here, sir, in a swallowtail coat evening dress and bowler hat, but it wouldn't do much good when I started sliding and slipping about trying to grab an old goose. Why, the other day I come here in me flannels and tried to catch that old bean goose and went arse over tip in a creek. I don't think brown overalls would be much good, sir."

But, despite the occasional rows, those were good days. Looking back on the Lighthouse, Kenzie says: "Peter Scott was a good boss and a good man. I've never had a better boss, though I reckon he underpaid me for that bean goose I caught him."

Nothing is forgotten in the mythology of the marshland. Even though Kenzie quite happily accepted the pound Scott paid him for the bird, twenty-five years later the matter is still on record.

"Do you know," says Kenzie, "the day after he paid me that pound I heard someone saying that goose was worth twenty pound."

Point out to Kenzie that the pound was possibly a bonus to a salaried employment and he would certainly spit in the nearest creek.

Throughout this phase Scott was shooting geese, as Kenzie says, "pretty heavy". The nicks which he cut in the stock of his twelve-bore wildfowling magnum for each goose it killed were creeping out towards the fore-end. He was punting pretty heavily also, often setting off at dawn in the double-handed twenty-two-foot punt with its eighteen-stone gun and returning late at night. It was Kenzie's job to maintain the equipment and clean up the bag, which sometimes numbered twenty or thirty ducks and geese. This employment made a sad hole in Kenzie's own sporting activities, for his boss did not expect him to be shooting also.

It came as a surprise, therefore, when Scott asked Kenzie to take him wigeon shooting one bitter night in 1937. It was in the middle of one of those blistering spells of freeze-up that can grip the Wash, The whole marsh had been frozen for six weeks, and succeeding tides had driven the ice-flows high up into the stalk edges and among the grasses on which the wigeon packs loved to feed. The birds were having a hard time, as they always do during prolonged frost. Whenever there was a partial thaw during the day, so that a shallow flash of water was created over their feeding grounds, the duck flighted onto it in great numbers as soon as night came. These flashes changed continually with the ebbs and flows of wind and frost, and Kenzie, despite his duties at the Lighthouse, usually knew where the best flighting points were.

On the night Scott suggested that Kenzie take him to the best wigeon ground everything was favourable. The wind was blowing half a gale full of snow-flakes and the clouds were scudding across the moon, so that it looked as though it was doing a hundred miles an hour through the sky. It is hopeless to shoot flighting duck against a clear sky and a full moon, for you never see your birds. This night the wind would keep them low and the clouds would silhouette them. The wigeon, moreover, were set on coming in, since they wanted to feed to their fill before the flash froze over again.

Scott and Kenzie split three boxes of cartridges, giving them about thirty-five each. When the flight started they didn't even need to take cover in a creek, so rough was the night.

"It was the only time I ever shot with Scott," remembers Kenzie, "and we was both shooting ver' ver' poor. We'd shot out by twelve-thirty in the morning when Scott had fourteen wigeon and I had seventeen."

Allowing for snow, darkness, and gale, many wildfowlers would not call this a bad proportion of kills per cartridge.

The pens at the Lighthouse were growing in size and number. By 1938 there were hundreds of birds there, including some exotic fowl like paradise shelduck, Australian shelduck, Emperor, cackling, and bar-headed geese. Among the commoner representatives were no fewer than sixty mallard. The value of the collection was considerable. Red-breasted geese, of which there were fifty-five, were even then worth £50 a pair. But there was little time ahead to enjoy the sight and sound of these birds.

When the War came Peter Scott went to take up his eventful and distinguished career in the Royal Navy, and the birds were evacuated, some to Ireland and some to enthusiasts and fanciers in Britain. Before he left the Lighthouse, Peter Scott shook Kenzie's hand and told him that he'd be back, and that when he returned he'd have the finest collection in the world. In fact, Scott never came back to Sutton Bridge after the War, but the second part of his prediction certainly came true.

Kenzie was still clearing things up at the Lighthouse in November 1939 when Annabel arrived from the north, escorted by five wild pinkfeet. Finding no other geese at home, she took her little skein away again.

Kenzie saw her once more when she came back on migration in 1940. This time she found neither anserine nor human inhabitants at the Lighthouse. She circled the pens five times and then carried on powerfully out to sea.

4

Kenzie was out of work. The next phase was entirely predictable. One night soon after the outbreak of war, Kenzie went into a pub. Arthur Porter who drove a lorry for the timber merchants was in the bar. "You want to come along with me tomorrow, Mac."

"Oh," said Kenzie suspiciously. "Why?"

"Because there's hundreds of pheasants where I'm going."

"All right. I don't mind."

Porter picked Kenzie up at seven-thirty the next morning. His lorry carried a big load of timber. Kenzie carried a double-barrelled fourten. Beyond King's Lynn, and on the way to Holt, Kenzie spotted six pheasants just the other side of a hedge.

"You ease up, Arthur," he said, "while I give these old birds one." He gave them three and stuffed three nice cocks under the front seat. Two miles further on he saw two more over the top of a brick wall. Arthur stopped and Kenzie climbed out, "snuck up", and "drawed back", and that was five under the seat. Close to Heacham he poked the gun through the window and "panned out" two more close by the hedgerow. He was just picking them up when he heard the lorry engine revving. Arthur Porter was waving frantically and shouting: "Mac! Come back, Mac! There's a copper. Oh my Gawd, there's a copper!"

Kenzie recalls with astonishment that he thought for a moment that Porter was going to drive away and leave him, but he ran after the moving lorry and managed to clamber aboard. The policeman was standing in the middle of the road. This was the first time he had been caught since the days of Jabus Dixon. Kenzie Thorpe's poaching luck had run out, and it was to be out for a very long time to come.

In this encounter, and in all the encounters that lay ahead—with the exception of one disastrous exchange much later in Kenzie's career—a ritual pattern emerges. In some respects it resembles classical ballet; the movements are recognized, the steps quite as formal. It might be more appropriate to compare it to the aggressive springtime display of the cock pheasant, for there, too, the moves are laid down by custom and blood is seldom actually drawn. It goes like this.

The Law makes its challenge. Kenzie makes a counterchallenge: this may take the form of faked aggression or of genuine flight. The Law refuses to be put off and pursues. Kenzie sees that the game is up and capitulates. He offers no more fight but relies on the most outrageous bluff, and this invariably fails.

Now the Law had challenged. "Drive at him, Arthur, knock him out of the way," ordered Kenzie. It is doubtful whether he meant the constable any real harm, any more than he had intended to shoot PC Dixon. He simply hoped that the chap would have the good sense to hop out of the way when he saw three tons of deal planks coming. The copper, to his credit, refused to budge, and Porter certainly wasn't going to risk a manslaughter charge. He stopped dead.

The Law opened the door on Kenzie's side. "Now, then. Where you from?"

This couldn't be bluffed out; the timber merchant's name was on the lorry.

"Sutton Bridge."

"Where's the pheasants?"

"What pheasants. We ain't shot none."

"That's quite all right. I seen everything."

Kenzie had hidden the birds but had left the butt end of the gun sticking out from under the seat. The policeman grabbed at it. When possession of a gun is threatened a minor display pattern reveals itself. It, too, is largely bluff, but it always calls for a struggle on Kenzie's part that stops short of real violence. Kenzie began to wrestle with the policeman, but, when he saw that this stout-hearted man meant business, he let him have the four-ten. But now Arthur Porter had started to cry. "I'll lose my job," he sobbed.

"He won't lose his job, will he, sir?" Kenzie asked the policeman, who can't really have been in any position to give reassurance. Nevertheless, he apparently felt, as did Kenzie, that the man needed comforting. Perhaps the "sir" coming close on the fight for the four-ten gun had helped.

"You'll be all right," the constable said to Porter. "You won't lose your job."

A week later, Kenzie got his summons. He had to appear in court over thirty miles away. The War was on and petrol was already in short supply. Kenzie approached Harry Usher up at the garage. "I've got a court do on, and I want to appear if I can."

"Okay," said Harry. "Cost you sixteen bob return."

Kenzie's appearance may have had something to do with the court's lack of sympathy. He turned up in a dressing-gown, carpet slippers, and an old pair of grey flannel trousers. The "do" cost him £7 and loss of gun. Arthur Porter didn't attend and he got away with a pound.

That night Kenzie met Porter in the local. "How did you git on?" Porter wanted to know.

"I didn't git on very well. They fined me seven pound. I pleaded for you and got you off."

Kenzie remembers bitterly: "Do you know, mild beer was fourpence a pint then? He treated me to just one, and didn't even say thank you."

Kenzie now got a job working on the new pumping station at Tydd. Here, for the first and last time in his life, he forsook the role of dedicated individualist and identified himself with the herd. He became a strike leader.

The rate for the job he was on was one and a penny an hour.

It was dirty, cold work and the men wanted one and three, which, they had heard, was the rate paid on other essential war work. The foreman, invoking some emergency order Kenzie had never dreamt of, told him that as a strike leader he could be locked up. Whether this was so or not, Kenzie could see that no career lay ahead for him at the pumping station.

He next joined a gang building pill-boxes along the sea wall.

This suited him very well, for the sea bank enclosed some of the best poaching lands in Lincolnshire. With his pill-box mates he found a form of leadership more suited to his talents. Not every man in his gang had a gun but every man could have a catapult. Kenzie made eight good, strong straight-shooters for the men on his lorry. He insisted on firing practice while the lorry was bowling along at thirty miles an hour between the various pill-box sites, and, under his tuition, progress was swift. As master gunner he delighted in demonstrating just how deadly the catapult could be in the right hands. At speed he shot at, and hit, the most improbable targets: a farm wife's milk can hanging up outside a kitchen window, an old oil lamp, from which he knocked all four panes of glass, on a post outside the church, and a gamekeeper's bicycle bell.

One day as they were driving along his brother Bob said: "Did you see that plate of apples in that cottage window, Kenzie?"

"No, I never."

"Well, you watch for it when we come back."

On the return journey along the same road Bob hissed : "Here it is now. Here it is now."

Kenzie's photographic memory recaptures this minor success:

"There were three plates of apples on that window-sill just tipped up at ten degrees, so I drawed back and went plank and knocked that centre plate straight out."

Bob was delighted. Soon after he had reason to curse Kenzie and his catapult. Taking their fire orders from their leader, the eight men had unloosed a volley at some roadside pheasants.

When the last elastic had twanged there were only seven men standing up in the lorry. Brother Bob was lying flat on his back with a bump the size of a turkey's egg swelling on his forehead.

Next morning exactly the same thing happened with another member of the syndicate.

Kenzie recalls the incident: "They weren't all very reliable shooters, so we packed up catapults, and I took the old twelve-bore goonn along instead. Cartridges were the trouble just then, it being the start of the war, so I was glad when Tom Hammond came along one day with some crow-skeering cartridges from Gedney Drove End. They was pretty rough stuff. I shot both barrels at an old pheasant and never touched a feather.

"I told Tom: 'They might skeer crows but they don't frighten pheasants.'

" 'Course they're all right,' Tom said.

"'All right,' I said. 'You knock over one of these here old cockerels.'

" 'I dursen't, the farmer might come out.'

"Tom wouldn't do it, so I shot at a cockerel and killed it stone dead.

" 'There you are,' said Tom, 'I told you they was all right.' "

By 1940, rationing was beginning to make itself felt. Kenzie decided that, provided he could get the cartridges, crow-scaring or otherwise, he would shoot everything he could sell. This gave him a pretty wide field, for almost anything on wings that carried a bit of flesh was negotiable. He was soon carting three barrow-loads of fowl up to the butcher's every week, and some very odd things that barrow carried. Bird protectionists as well as gastronomes might be horrified at some of the entries on the barrow's passenger list. There were brent geese (10s. each), shelduck (4s.), sea-gulls (6d.), gadwall (2s.), reeves (9d.), water-hens (1s.), black-tailed godwits (9d.), as well as run of the mill quarry such as pheasants (£2 a brace), partridges (8s.), woodcock (3s.), hares (10s.), and wood-pigeons (4s.). Cartridges came from all sorts of sources, regular and irregular. The RAF always had a fair supply for training air gunners. It is doubtful whether any of the trainees subsequently hit as many airborne targets as did Kenzie Thorpe.

In '41 there came a break in Kenzie's shooting activities, though fortunately it occurred during the off-season. Kenzie was called up for the Navy. He passed his medical and set off for Felixstowe. The date was June 9. The life there suited him well and, despite his experience in the schooner *Alert*, he was looking forward to going to sea again.

Then, one afternoon, his mess was called on parade for saluting drill. When it came to "hup-two-three", Kenzie could get his hand "hup", but his fingers refused to "two-three" to the regulation position. They remained curled. The blow his mother had struck him on the funny bone with the dust-pan has left him unable to use the fingers of his right hand normally, but this, as has been demonstrated, has never curtailed an active life. The Chief Petty Officer spotted the curled fingers and ordered him to fall out. Kenzie asked the Chief, who was a friend of his, not to report the injury, but the CPO said that he had no choice.

Kenzie spent six weeks on the sick list doing nothing except running a fairly profitable dhobi business. The doctors wanted to operate, but Kenzie, with the countryman's natural distrust of surgery applied to anything as basic as a limb, declined. A few days after this refusal he was mustered at the ship's office and trotted in at the double.

"Thorpe," said the Captain, "I can offer you a shore-based job here. You can move your wife and family up. Frankly you're not going to be any use to the Navy in an active role."

"Do I have any choice, sir?"

"No, I'm afraid not. You're medically unfit. Able Seaman Thorpe, the medical board recommends that you be discharged. You are discharged the Service."

Kenzie recalls: "I went out of that office, *and* the Royal Navy, faster than what I went in. They gave me a suit, an oilskin and a cap, and my messmates had a whip round for the kids. Two days later I was on my way back to Sutton Bridge."

The date was August 8. In four more days the duck-shooting season would be open. If the Navy didn't want him, all right. They might not consider him fit for active service, but Kenzie had other ideas. Now he could start shooting in earnest.

Nineteen forty-two was Kenzie Thorpe's record year. His bag was as follows. September: 77 head, mostly partridges and hares. October: 108 head, including 15 mallard, 9 wigeon, 24 partridges and 18 pheasants. November: 185 head, among which were 76 mallard, 72 wigeon, 7 geese. December: 183 head, a mixed bag this, with pheasants numbering 81, geese 40, wigeon 52, and shelduck 20. January produced 146 wigeon, 25 geese, 43 shelduck, 11 curlew, the total for the month being 257. February wasn't so bad either: 45 geese, 137 shelduck, 65 wigeon, 15 mallard, 2 curlew, 1 hare, and 1 swan.

There were some highlights in this mixed shooting of which any wildfowler, or even game-shot, might have been proud. Kenzie was still getting visits from some of his old wildfowling customers when on leave. Kenneth Bromley was one.

Bromley, Kenzie has described, as "a real hard case. Every hair on his head was a strand of rope yarn. Every spot of blood in his body Stockholm tar. He didn't feel the cold, nor frost, nor nothing. Nothing put him off his wildfowling, and he turned out to be a very good wildfowler indeed and a very good shot."

Only a real hard case would have turned up that January of 1942 in Sutton Bridge, having driven up from Kent in an old Austin Seven on scrounged petrol. The marsh was gripped by snow and ice and it was blowing like the devil from the east.

The first evening Kenzie took Bromley out onto Terrington Marsh just as dusk was falling. It was a very wild night, and the snow was packed hard on the upper part of the saltings. They settled into creeks among the crab grass where there were a few open pools, and soon they had begun to shoot "very strong". A lot of the wigeon fell on the crab grass and disappeared through the frozen crust, powdered snow closing behind them so that they were never found. After a couple of hours Bromley had shot out of cartridges. Kenzie had twenty-five left. It was plain to both of them that if they had had a proper supply this could have been a very big flight indeed. It was equally certain that, if the weather held, it would be exactly the same the next night with the wigeon piling in from the sea for shelter and food. They counted their birds. Kenzie had forty-five and Bromley twenty-four, with possibly another twenty unpicked beneath the snow. Kenzie suggested that they call it a night, keep the twenty-five cartridges in reserve for tomorrow and try to rake together some more in the morning. About the latter Kenzie was not very hopeful. They had some hot rum and soup, piled into the Austin Seven and drove back to bed, Kenzie at home, and Bromley in the Bridge Hotel, the traditional Sutton Bridge wildfowler's pub. Kenzie was hardly in bed when he heard a pounding at the door. It was Bromley.

"Kenzie, I've had a bit of luck."

"You haven't, sir."

"I have. Mother's sent me five hundred Purdey cartridges and I've come round to give you a present of a hundred."

"That's very, very thoughtful of you, Mr Bromley. I'll tell you what we'll do: we'll give the morning flight a miss and go out and belt the old wigeon properly tomorrow night on Terrington Marsh."

The next night it was even more blastingly cold. They got to the marsh about 4.30, just as it was falling dark. It was hard to stand in the cutting east wind and the sky was livid with snow. They separated to their positions of the previous night. Hardly had they done so when eight brent geese lifted out of a creek close to Bromley. Kenzie heard a double shot and saw one of the black geese fall out of the sky. One of the survivors headed towards Kenzie. He was just about to put his gun up when it "panned out" dead as a stone and fell at his feet.

Kenzie settled down in his creek. He was wearing a green oilskin, a scarf, a "Ballyhava" hat, several sweaters, sea-boots and thick stockings, and at that moment he needed every layer of warmth. He got ready to wait for the flight with the box of a hundred cartridges open in front of him on the creek bank, the lid propped up to keep flying snow-flakes off the ammunition. He kept the wind at his back so that the wigeon would come in towards him, and he sat looking out over the flash to which he hoped they would flight. Hardly had the last light drained from the sky when the first bunch appeared. They circled once then swooped in fast and low with paddles down. Kenzie's first shot punched three out of the party. Remembering his experience of the night before he doubled out of the creek to pick them before they disappeared through the snow crust. As he was gathering them, some more steadied to pitch. He had three dead birds in one hand and a gun with one loaded cartridge in the left barrel. He fired one-handed and brought another wigeon down. Then, as fast as he shot birds, he laid them out as decoys, their light breast feathers upwards to entice others out of the sky. The pile of empty cartridges in the creek bottom grew fast, and, as they did so, Kenzie performed a wildfowler's strip-tease. He got so hot running to recover his birds that he was soon down to his shirt and still sweating.

Sometime before midnight the hundredth spent Purdey case fell into the mud. Kenzie put down his gun, and, amid wigeon still determined to land, he made his count. His one hundred cartridges had produced sixty-three wigeon.

He could no longer hear shots from Bromley's direction and guessed that he had probably packed up and made for the car. The problem now was to get sixty-three wigeon, weighing on an average 2 1/2 lb, back the

A snapshot of Bob Ashby and Kenzie with a mixed bag
outside Kenzie's council house at Sutton Bridge.
Photo by courtesy of Bob Ashby.

mile and a half to the rendezvous. He loaded twenty-five birds into his rucksack, took off his cartridge belt and removed the twenty-five reserve cartridges from it. Then he tucked twenty wigeon beaks in instead, the necks and bodies of the birds hanging between belt and himself. He next tore up a handkerchief and tied wigeon together in bunches of four with the linen strips. These he hung on his arms and over his gun barrels. At last, he began to plod off the marsh very very slowly. When he was a quarter of a mile from the car he heard Bromley hoot.

"I loosed the wigeon down and give him a bugle down the barrel of my gun, and soon Bromley came out to help. He took over the rucksack. He had forty-two wigeon and the two brent geese, and I had sixty-three. That was my record shoot at wigeon, and believe me when we got to the car I was ver' ver' warm."

Kenzie's brother Verdon, who never took seriously to shooting or poaching, sometimes came out with him on the marsh about this time. Verdon had never shot a goose and Kenzie promised to supply him with one. One night in 1942, soon after the record wigeon shoot, the Thorpes were creeping along the top of the sea wall close to Shep White's cottage, now demolished, at the Holbeach St Matthew end of the marsh. Suddenly the geese started to come in off the sea. Kenzie stood and listened and judged that they were pitching not far inland on G. K. Thompson's farm.

"Come on," he said to Verdon, "let's go and stir the old sods up."

"You're never going in there, boy," said Verdon, who was comparatively law-abiding and knew Thompson's keeper as a lively and conscientious man.

"I am, boy," said Kenzie. "Come on."

The geese were feeding under the moon on a potato field.

Kenzie built rough hides out of potato tops, then he began to call, and the geese came nicely. His first salvo brought down a right and left, and Verdon had soon bagged his first pinkfoot. For three hours the brothers lay on their stomachs behind the potato tops and the score mounted to thirteen geese. With his eyes at ground level, Kenzie could see right across the field in the moonlight. Suddenly, on the far side, he noticed a pair of black objects. He hissed to Verdon to hold his fire and both Thorpes lay silent. By and by, the two objects disappeared, so Kenzie began to call again, but now he noticed that the geese only flew half-way up the field towards the dead birds he had propped up as decoys. There they checked and swerved away. "Hullo," thought Kenzie, "wonder what's made them shy off?" Soon he knew. The two black objects had worked a flanker on him and were right up to Verdon's position. A few seconds later he saw them pull Verdon to his feet and hold him up at gunpoint. Kenzie ran across.

"Who the hell are you?" "Home Guard."

"Home Guard!" said Kenzie with great scorn. "I thought you were supposed to be defending us against invasion, not spoiling an Englishman's sport. Any road, what you got that rifle on my brother for, and that fixed bayonet, and that revolver? If you'll put down them guns, I've a good mind to give you a bloody good walloping."

"Never mind that talk," said one of the Home Guards, and this may have taken a bit of courage, for Kenzie's gun was at least loaded; "let's see your identification papers."

"You can see those," agreed Kenzie.

The other Home Guard said: "I think we ought to take them up to the foreman's place."

Kenzie laughed. "If you're going to do that," he said slowly, "it'll take you and all the Home Guard in England." To Verdon he said: "Come on, boy, they ain't got nothing else to do now the pubs is closed." And the Thorpes gathered up their geese and stalked off in the direction of the sea wall, leaving the defenders of England temporarily nonplussed.

Kenzie was shaking with indignation, but Verdon who was, you may remember, no bigger than six penn'orth of coppers, was shaking with fright. When they mounted their bikes and rode off, Verdon pedalled so fast to get away from the scene of the crime that Kenzie had to shout to him to slow up. As it turned out there was nothing to be gained from speed, for Kenzie now spotted that a policeman had cut off their escape along the bank towards Sutton Bridge. "Turn round," ordered Kenzie, "we'll get out at Shep White's." But they hadn't pedalled far on their return trip when twelve Home Guards with fixed bayonets stepped out from behind a hedge and forced them off their machines. Kenzie saw that the posse was reinforced by three farmers whose fields he regularly poached, G. K. Thompson, Worth and Caudwell.

Thompson, whose land he had been on that night, said: "Now then, Kenzie, what you been doing?"

"Nothing, sir, just been after these old geese, that's all."

"You'd better open up your bag."

So the geese were tipped out on the sea wall, but no pheasants, and no hares, and this was obviously a surprise to all present.

One of the Home Guard piped up with: "I say, sir, if he shot those geese on your land can't you claim them?"

Kenzie saw that this character didn't understand the law, or at least the local version of it. "No, he can't," he said. "Them geese ain't game. They're wildfowl, and they're mine, and that's that."

Mr Thompson never challenged this statement, and the Thorpes were allowed to pick up their geese again. There was no need to take names and addresses. It would have been like the Marshal of Tombstone asking Jessie James where he lived.

Once again the Thorpe brothers rode off.

"We're going to be nabbed for sure," said Verdon.

"Nah," said Kenzie, "we didn't have no game." He suddenly stopped his bike. "Hold hard," he said. "Hark at that ... geese."

"Come on," urged Verdon. "They've pitched on Caudwell's."

"Leave 'em there."

"Not likely. Let's go and brown into them."

"We've had one do with the police," pleaded Verdon.

"They'll think we've packed up."

Kenzie, dismounted and led the way. At the end of a long stalk up a dyke they got within range and the geese jumped. Verdon was uneasy and so missed with both barrels, but Kenzie's shot dropped a pinkfoot.

When they got back to the bikes there was Caudwell, this time along with his gamekeeper and a policeman.

"Well, Kenzie," said farmer Caudwell, "we've caught you twice tonight. I reckon that's a fair cop."

Kenzie didn't argue, but kept hold of his goose.

Two weeks later the brothers were summoned. They were found guilty of night poaching and were fined £7.10s. each. The fourteen geese had fetched them £7, so they were well down on the night.

The injustice of the thing irritates twenty-odd years later. "We was never after game," Kenzie complains. "All the police could talk about in court was pheasants. They never mentioned the geese."

Other wartime trespasses after geese were more successful and one in particular deserves special mention. Indeed it was such a perfect operation that it has been referred to ever since as The Light Railway Night. It is important in one other respect for it introduces a character who was to play a large part in Kenzie's poaching activities—Horry.

Most of Kenzie's poaching companions since the early days with Ernie Burton had been unsatisfactory. His brothers were either insufficiently keen or too nervous. Others with whom he had paired briefly lacked team spirit. They were greedy, or just didn't have the right approach to the business, namely that though poaching is a business it is first and foremost a sport.

Horry—full name Horace Savage—fulfilled all these requirements. Horry Savage is a small man, greyish at the temples, quick of movement and possessed of a surprisingly loud voice. As a poaching ally, he wasn't a brilliant shot, though he was adequate, but he would go anywhere and do anything. He had gun and would travel. He remained cool, though he was inclined to be talkative in the excitement of the chase. But above all he had the same cops and robbers approach to each enterprise that Kenzie had.

They had met first some time before the War when Kenzie was snooping along the sea bank looking for hares. There he saw this man, in broad daylight, walking a farmer's potato field for pheasants. Now this, in a heavily keepered area, took a bit of nerve, so Kenzie "snuck down" into a dyke to watch events, and intercept anything the lone hand put up and missed. He watched with admiration while the other man knocked down a couple of cock pheasants, and then Kenzie himself bowled over two hares that Horry Savage had started. He had a long shot at a covey of partridges that Horry had flushed and missed, and soon Horry had worked to the end of the field. Kenzie showed himself. Neither was in any doubt what the other was. "We got," recalls Kenzie, "into very deep conversation at once." It was a meeting of, well, if not soul mates, then at least of the right and left barrels from the same gun. The foundation of an ideal partnership was sealed with Horry's invitation to take a trip out together shortly.

As an experiment in teamwork this first poaching expedition was a marked success. Horry showed himself to be almost as much of an expert on the doings of hares as Kenzie himself. It was one of those thick rime-frost mornings, and as they walked together down the sea wall, Horry looked at the signs in the frosted grass.

"I think there're a few old heers about here," he said to Kenzie. They drove the bank carefully and shot nineteen. Despite the fact that they had three miles to walk with the bag they were "ver' ver' pleased", an expression which, when used by Kenzie, means the ultimate in pleasure or success. He is even willing to add a testimonial to Horry when he remembers that first trip together. "Horry," he says, "is a good old sport. He'll go anywhere, do anything, though he's a little chap. He's been poaching with me ever since. The biggest bag of pheasants we ever had together was ninety-three in three nights, and then it would have been more if we hadn't been 'sturbed off."

On the Light Railway Night their minds were set on geese. Kenzie had discovered that the pinkfeet were feeding on Ward's farm, two and a half miles inland from the sea wall at the Shep White's, that is to say, at the Holbeach end, of the marsh. There was no moon up in the early part of the evening, so they didn't get into position until eight. Because they were trespassing and might want to make a quick getaway Kenzie had brought no decoys. He intended to rely on skilful calling of the geese by mouth. He found precisely where the geese had been feeding and then placed Horry and himself in a dyke with the wind at their backs.

About nine, just as the moon came up, the first geese started flying around. Kenzie called as hard as he knew how but the geese were wary, flying half-way up the field but refusing to approach and pitch by the dyke.

"I wish I had some 'coys," he said to Horry. "Here, have you got any paper?"

"I've got my sandwich wrappings and an old newspaper. Why?"

Kenzie tore up the paper into ovals slightly larger than goose size and set the pieces out, each with a clod of earth to give it body and weight it down. Then he hid himself again and began to call.

"The geese," he recalls, "came lovely. We got two out of the first skein, and, of course, put these out as decoys. And for the next hour or two we was shooting ver' ver' strong. By midnight we had twenty-five geese. The problem was how to carry them home. Then I remembered there was a light railway the contractors had been using for carting stuff to the sea wall defences. So we tied the geese to our guns and carried them to the shed where they kept the railway trucks and soon had one out. We loaded the geese and ourselves on to the trucks and sat on the back in the moonlight, pushing with our feet. And we didn't have to push hard for the wind blew us all the way two and a half miles to the sea wall where our bikes were, and we didn't have to work hardly at all really. And that's what I call real gentleman's goose shooting."

Extracts from Mackenzie Thorpe's game-book during the War years:

1941: 169 pheasants, 59 partridges, 45 hares, 44 geese, 12 mallard, 147 wigeon, 32 shelduck, 25 rabbits, 16 green plover, 22 curlew, 17 sea-gulls (various), 4 knot, 5 moorhens, 2 coot, 1 greenshank, 1 jay, 5 crows, 1 weasel, 1 sparrow hawk, 4 whimbrel, 3 godwit, 5 redshank.

1942: 48 pheasants, 72 partridges, 68 hares, 1 woodcock, 106 geese, 146 mallard, 231 wigeon, 193 shelduck, 2 shoveller, 1 tufted, 61 plover, 18 pigeon, 79 redshank, 50 knot, 40 curlew, 1 reeve, 1 gadwall, 1 pintail, 1 black-tailed godwit, 2 whimbrel, 6 rabbits.

1943: 42 pheasants, 67 partridges, 82 hares, 316 wigeon, 53 mallard, 45 grey geese, 1 brent goose, 86 curlew, 50 gulls, 9 crows, 10 shelducks, 34 pigeon, 73 plover, 40 redshank, 55 knot.

5

THE PARTNERSHIP WITH Horry Savage soon became firmly established. From 1943 until 1949 they roamed Norfolk and Lincolnshire together, shooting for the pot (and, admittedly, for profit, as the wartime meat shortage became more acute), but poaching mainly because they couldn't resist it. Kenzie's luck with the law, once broken, seemed to fail him repeatedly.[1] When Kenzie was caught, Horry was often caught with him. On many trips, though, they got away with it. For a long time they got away with it with the swans, which were then fetching 30s. each, and of which, in Kenzie's and Horry Savage's view, there were far too many. Kenzie certainly anticipated the school of

---

[1] Between March 1931 and June 1956, Kenzie was convicted (often with Horry) on twenty-nine charges connected with poaching. His fines and costs totalled £120. 17s. 9d., and he lost four guns by confiscation. Offences ranged from killing game on a Sunday to inflicting grievous bodily harm. But note that 1956 is the last date in this record of crime.

thought that today advocates the rigid control of mute swans. Between the years 1943 and 1946 he accounted for 250 of them. Kenzie and Horry made their first attack in 1943 at Counter Drain on the River Glen. This was the other side of Spalding from Sutton Bridge and a good sixteen-mile cycle ride.

They arrived at Counter Drain station armed with a .410 gun late one Saturday afternoon. An aged railway porter met them. "Hullo, old feller," said Kenzie, "seen any swans about?"

"There's hoondreds on 'em," said the ancient man. "Why?"

Why is a question asked sooner or later by everyone in these parts. It is part of the natural suspicion of other people's motives that seems woven into the Lincolnshire fenman's mind.

"'Cos we want to take some photographs of them," Kenzie explained.

"Well, I hope you git some good ones." "I hope we do too," said Kenzie.

They took the gun off the bike and fitted it together. Then they climbed the embankment and looked down into the river. There was only one swan to be seen and Kenzie shot it. The Glen was very twisty just there, so he sent Horry over the bridge to walk any swans he might find up to him. Almost at once he heard Horry shouting in a voice that always seemed to Kenzie ridiculously loud for a fairly small fellow: "Cor, there's hundreds of 'em!"

"No!" Kenzie shouted back. This again is a standard reaction to any startling but as yet unconfirmed piece of news.

"There is. Hundreds."

Soon the swans came swimming round the bend with Horry behind shooing them. There were twenty-five. Kenzie started "panning them out". He shot six and then, hearing shouts from the station, judged it was time to be moving on. It was already getting dark so they packed the swans, three in one bag and four in another, and set off to ride the sixteen miles home. Kenzie was carrying a powerful torch, for obvious reasons, and, as they rode through Spalding in the wartime blackout, he was using it as a headlight. They were riding along by the river, which runs beside the main street in Spalding, when the torch picked out something white.

"There's another," said Kenzie.

"Another what?"

"Swan, of course. Wait a mo'. I'll torch him."

Kenzie abandoned his bike and grabbed the swan by the neck.

Then he pulled it up onto the main road and flung himself on it in a cloud of feathers. Bird and man wrestled together for several minutes, and then the swan joined its three dead companions in one of the bags.

"Eight," said Kenzie as he mounted again. "Not a bad day's work."

Their luck held fairly well into 1944, although they had a near thing with farmer Ward's keeper. This time they were out after geese (trespassing, naturally), Kenzie with an eight-bore and Horry with a twelve. It was past midnight on a blustery January night when Kenzie heard Horry's excited voice above the gale:

"Hurry up, old feller, there's somebody coming."

"Send him along to me," ordered Kenzie. He pulled his hood up quickly so that only part of his face was showing, and awaited the onslaught.

Kenzie Thorpe has a very pronounced gift for mimicry. It is evident in his extraordinary ability to imitate geese and call waders, and equally to assume other accents, especially posh ones. His experiences with Peter Scott and his friends had given him plenty of opportunities for studying standard public school English. Now he chose a cut-glass voice.

"Who are you, my man?" he asked the intruder.

"I'm Mr Ward's gamekeeper," a piece of information that came as no surprise at all.

"Ward," said Kenzie, "Ward? I thought this was Faulkner's farm. I have permission to shoot Faulkner's farm for geese."

He was, perhaps, overdoing the accent now, for the keeper said suspiciously: "Faulkner's farm is miles from here. What's your name?"

Kenzie thought: "If this hood slips he'll know it right enough," but he said calmly: "My name's John Winter, and I've just come through from Cambridge." (Memories of Scott. Winter had been a sailing companion of Scott's in the Lighthouse days.)

"Oh, have you?" said the keeper doubtfully. "And what's your friend's name?"

Perhaps it was the strain of simultaneously keeping up the accent and the hood, but invention suddenly flagged. "I don't know his name. You'd better ask him."

Then, realizing that the bluff was wearing mighty thin, he added: "Look here, old boy, we'll go off without any trouble. If you come back in daylight you'll find several geese lying around for yourself which we haven't picked up yet."

The keeper wasn't really interested in geese. With some justification he was worried for his pheasants. This, and the fact that there were two poachers and the night was a dark and wild one on which a case of assault and battery would pass unmarked, possibly prompted him to let the trespassers go off "without any trouble". But he followed them at a safe distance just to make sure they did leave the premises.

Horry was jubilant. As they stalked off the field he shouted to Kenzie: "When I heard you tell him your name was John Winter I thought of telling him my name was John Summer. Oh gawd," he broke off, "that damn' keeper's right behind us."

"Well, he can't fail to have heard you. Come on, let's run for it."

They reached Horry's little Austin Seven well ahead of the keeper. The engine started at the first touch and they were away.

The old Austin Seven was not always so obliging. It let them down disastrously at Sandringham some time later. Poaching the King's coverts was a notion which had haunted Kenzie since his first abortive attempt as a fourteen-year-old. With Horry by his side he felt that he couldn't fail. But he was wrong.

This time the armament was a .410 and a .22 rifle made in 1900, the latter, according to Kenzie, "a lovely shooting gun and dead silent". They drove out in the late afternoon and scored early in the proceedings with a cock pheasant which Kenzie shot from the front of the Austin Seven as the bird was trying to nip through a wire fence. He hid it in the usual storage place in this vehicle, a cubby-hole in front of the spare wheel. It was still too light to go into full action, so they pulled up on top of West Newton Hill, which is under a mile from Sandringham House, and sat in the car to watch the pheasants going up to roost. Horry was just lighting a cigarette and pausing to observe that there seemed to be a nice lot of birds about when a Land-Rover came swishing down the road. When it got close it stopped, almost blocking the exit route.

"Leave this to me," Kenzie told Horry.

Two men jumped out of the Land-Rover, one a big elderly fellow and the other much younger. There was no doubt who they were and what they wanted. These were the Royal keepers.

"Hullo," said the big man, "what's your business?"

"Can you tell me," countered Kenzie, "whether this is the right road for Sandringham?"

"You don't have to ask that, do you?" said the big man.

"We're going to search the car."

"You can't," Kenzie said, "you're not constables. You're just keepers."

It was a good legal point, but not, apparently, good enough, for the older man said: "I'm Mr Amos, the King's head keeper, and I'm also a police constable."

Kenzie was now sure that the game was up. All he wanted to do was to save the guns and particularly the .22 rifle, which he still held between his knees. He played for time. "Can I see your identity card as a constable?" he asked Amos. While the keeper was producing it, Kenzie climbed out of the Austin and dropped the .22 rifle into some long grass. Unfortunately there wasn't quite enough grass to cover it. The younger keeper had by now found the .410 under the front seat but hadn't come upon the cock pheasant.

Kenzie grabbed the gun from him and said: "You can't take that. We ain't been poaching." He threw the .410 back into the car. The keepers hadn't yet found any evidence of poaching and there was still, in Kenzie's view, time to make a getaway. With luck Horry could just edge past the Land-Rover. "Come on," he ordered Horry, "let's get out of it."

But this time the Austin Seven wouldn't start. Worse, the keepers had spotted the rifle lying in the grass. Kenzie jumped out of the car and dived at it. The keepers dived, too, and all three were on the ground with a hold on the gun. They fought for several seconds and then the younger keeper let go and jumped on Kenzie's back. At this Kenzie released Amos and the rifle to throw off his assailant. Amos, unopposed, now had the rifle, and the battle was lost.

Considering the set-to, they all parted fairly amicably, but the summonses arrived for Horry and Kenzie as usual. The bill ultimately delivered to them at Grimston Court two months later was quite extensive. Items included: confiscation of rifle, £1 for possession of a fire-arm without certificate, £5 for coming from land in pursuit of game, £4 for trespassing, and £1 for opposing a constable.

Even now Kenzie still complains of the injustice of certain aspects of the affair. "Amos," he says bitterly, "was not a constable. He was only a *special* constable."

There were others at the game, too, and sometimes poaching parties ran into each other in the darkness. Such was the case one dark night on Caudwell's Farm when Kenzie and Horry were doing a quick check-up on farmer Caudwell's trees for roosting birds. While he was crouching at the base of a tall oak trying to get a bird silhouetted on a bough, Kenzie spotted two, presumably hostile, black objects against the sky.

"My mind," he recalls, "worked ver' ver' quick. I called out: 'Halt! Who goes there?' There was a lot of Home Guard about in those days. And back comes a rough, old voice bellowing: 'Never mind who we are. Who the hell are you?'"

One man in the other party now made a quick getaway, leaving the owner of the ancient voice to face whatever Kenzie and Horry might turn out to be, alone. Kenzie wanted to reassure the lone operator.

"I know who you are, old feller," he called sociably.

The opposition wasn't taking any chances. "Never mind who I am, just you come any closer and you're going to get this."

"Pack it up," said Kenzie. "You're Whiskers Burton."

"And what if I am? Who the hell are you?"

"Kenzie."

"Well, why didn't you say so? I came close to shooting you."

Kenzie chuckled, though he didn't doubt the truth of this. Remembering the incident, he describes Whiskers Burton as "a real hard old case, a Drove Ender. Whiskers was then sixty-seven. He stood only four-foot-six and was as thin as a heron. He didn't care for the biggest man in England and he was always fighting in the pubs. What's more," Kenzie adds with genuine admiration, "he could stand on his head on a pint glass. And that was Whiskers Burton. His real name was Matty, and he'd got five pheasants that night, and good luck to him."

Fines were one thing. Prison was another. Kenzie Thorpe's approach to keepers and policemen had so far always been reasonably consistent. In essence this was that you should bluff, bluster, flee, wrestle a little if necessary, but never aim or land a blow that might be described later as assault. Kenzie went poaching for the sheer thrill it gave him, quite apart from any money he might later make from selling the bag, and the same was true of Horry Savage. He genuinely held that keepers and constables had a job to do and that it would not be within what he conceived to be the rules of the game if they collected a bloody nose or a black eye while doing it. The affair of Keeper Sellers, therefore, is somewhat surprising, until you learn that there was a fenland feud at the back of it.

One foggy January morning in 1945, Kenzie went round to Horry's place and remarked that the weather was very nice and just right for a run out after a few hares. Horry agreed that the fog looked like lying all day. They decided to try Worth's estate over at Holbeach Hurn. After a brisk cycle ride they started in straight away, Horry walking the first batch of fields towards Kenzie who was soon shooting "very strong". After a couple of drives Horry was sweating so hard, despite the chill air, that he suggested that Kenzie walk the next one. Kenzie agreed, but just then he noticed two men approaching. He went down on one knee to get a better sight of them against the fog and saw that one had a stick and a mackintosh and looked every inch a keeper.

"Come over this way, Bill," he called to Horry. But the man in the mac came too.

Kenzie decided on bluster: "Who the hell are you?"

"I'm Worth's keeper, Mr Sellers."

"Oh, are you?" said Kenzie. "In that case you're just the man I've been wanting to meet. What are you going to do about this here job?"

"I'm going to report you," said the keeper.

"Oh," said Kenzie, "then I'll give you something to put in your report." With that he very deliberately unloaded his gun, put the gun down, and took hold of the keeper by his collar.

"What did you say you were going to do?" he demanded.

"I'm going to report you," said the keeper with, one can't help feeling, a fair measure of courage.

With that Kenzie let him go and put a straight left on his jaw. The keeper got up twice and each time Kenzie showed him a bit of the form that once belonged to the middle-weight champion of Lincolnshire. Keeper Sellers stayed down for the count on the third knock-down.

"Come on, Horry," said Kenzie, "let's get out on it."

They made off towards their cycles, but on the way Kenzie heard geese murmuring in the fog, and fog is the weather in which they are most easily called. He brought them in once and they both got off a couple of barrels without success. Possibly the encounter with Sellers and its totally unforeseen outcome had affected their aim, but on the whole this seems doubtful.

When they reached the main road and started to pedal home they heard a car approaching and slowing as it crept up behind in the fog. They didn't look round. Both thought that this was it. But it was only a friend offering a lift. Neither said a word about the encounter with the keeper either to the driver of the car or to anyone back home at Sutton Bridge.

The assault took place on a Monday. The next day, Horry and Kenzie were due to go off to Thorney on a sort of winter poaching holiday. They had heard nothing from the police. Perhaps, Kenzie told himself, but without much real conviction, the fog had concealed their identity.

The expedition to Thorney was a great success. They slept most of the daylight hours away in a stable and went torching at night. At the end of twenty-four hours the bag was: twenty hares, eight geese, two pheasants, and five pigeons. They loaded the swag on to their cycles and biked home eighteen miles at a pace which Kenzie describes as "nice and comfortable".

Mrs Thorpe greeted Kenzie with the news that the police had been. This was nothing exceptional, and she laid no particular stress on it, except to add that they were coming back.

"Oh," said Kenzie. This undoubtedly *was* it.

The Superintendent arrived shortly afterwards.

"Now then, Kenzie," he began, "what did you hit Worth's keeper, Sellers, for on Monday?"

"I don't know what you're talking about. I wasn't anywhere near Worth's place on Monday."

"Sellers knows you well enough. We've no doubt about you. Now you might as well come clean. Who's this Bill?"

"Bill? I don't go poaching with no Bill."

But it can only have been a routine question for the names Thorpe and Savage were indissolubly linked in police minds and police records. Next day the Superintendent took keeper Sellers down to

Horace Savage's house and the keeper identified him by the grey in his side whiskers. The assault had taken place on December 16, 1945. The case came up almost a month later to the day.

Horry was fined £2 for trespassing in pursuit of game with £2 costs. So was Kenzie, but the magistrates had had enough. For causing grievous bodily harm to Sellers, Kenzie was sentenced to three months in gaol.

This was something which Kenzie had not foreseen. The full shock of what was to happen to him, right in the middle of the best shooting weather of the year, only hit him as the constable led him down from the dock. All the same, it seemed to him that hitting Sellers had been worth it. The exact nuances of the situation between the two men are hard to recapture sharply at this distance in time. In some way, though, Kenzie felt that there was a matter of family honour at stake. Sellers had, in Kenzie's estimation, deeply offended his mother by offering her ten shillings after she had done all the laying-out after the death of his, Sellers's, mother. Also Sellers had caught Verdon poaching. Verdon must from all accounts have been pretty easy to catch, what with his diminutive stature, general lack of shooting ability and poaching zest, and total absence of any sense of direction. Kenzie no doubt felt protective towards his younger brother. Sellers had caught him shooting rabbits and Verdon had lost his .410 and had been fined £5. This to the impartial observer seems well within a keeper's rights and even duty, but, put with the affair of the laying-out, it apparently added up for Kenzie to an affront to his family which he personally felt bound to avenge. It may not seem logical but things like this happen in the Fens. And now he was going to gaol in payment for three cleansing, though seemingly unjustifiable, straight lefts.

Kenzie was taken from court to Lincoln prison in a Black Maria. The impact of what prison meant, even for three months, engulfed him when they hustled him out of the van and he found himself looking up at the high walls and tall dark gates. A small wicket opened in the big doors and a prison officer pushed him through with the dread words "lead on". The wicket gate slammed behind. He remembers that he felt as though he had been jammed inside a big black bottle with the cork squeezed home tight behind him. Lincoln gaol was a long way from the salt marsh.

He was told to strip. The doctor examined him, and he was ordered to take a bath. The water was stone cold. That didn't worry him, but, when he was led back to the cell in which he had taken off his clothes, he saw that his own suit had been replaced by a grey prison outfit. "That," recalls Kenzie, "shook me more than anything that happened." Another "screw" arrived and said, "Lead on." This time the walk took him to a cell. He was pushed inside and the door shut on him. Kenzie looked round the place. It was bare. There was no knob to the inside of the door, no bed or bedding. The only furniture was a small table in the corner. Kenzie had been out goose shooting the two previous nights, and was tired, so he decided to get his head down. But the concrete floor was too cold. He climbed up and looked through the barred window into the yard but could see no one, nor could he hear another soul. He formed the impression that he was the only prisoner in the gaol.

At last, when it was getting dark, a warder opened the door and uttered the nightmare words "lead on". Kenzie led, this time to another cell. "Get in there," said the warder. Kenzie hesitated. "Get on, you know the way." Kenzie wanted to tell the screw that this was his first day and that he didn't know the ropes, but he was too cowed to argue. The door of this second cell slammed on him, and here, he saw straightaway, was a distinct improvement. There was a bedboard with three blankets, a washbasin, a chamber pot, and a chair. He stuck the chair against the window and looked out on the yard. It was getting dark now, and the place was still deathly silent. In these circumstances sleep seemed the obvious thing, so he made the rough bed and climbed into it.

No sooner had he settled down than a grating shot back and a voice bellowed through the door: "What you doing in there? Get out of that bed. How long you been in here?"

"I've only been in here tonight, sir."

"Oh, have you? Well, if you're in that bed tomorrow night, you'll be pegged."

Since he hadn't been told to get up in so many words, Kenzie stayed in bed, but an hour or so later he heard a bell ring and the noise of the other prisoners making their beds.

When morning came Kenzie made his as neatly as he knew how, but when the cell door opened and the screw came in, he took one look at it and sent for the man in the next cell to show Kenzie the correct method of prison kit lay-out.

This lag had three years to do, and plainly regarded Thorpe with his three months as the merest amateur. He told Kenzie that he would certainly get one month remitted if he behaved himself.

A pleasantly relaxed club-like atmosphere now set in. The cell doors remained open so that the prisoners could fetch water. Kenzie washed himself and decided that he preferred privacy. So he shut his cell door himself. This earned him another rebuke. Apparently you couldn't lock yourself in if you wanted to, even in gaol. The door was opened again for breakfast. Kenzie's cell neighbour poked his head in and whispered: "Save me your porridge."

"What!" said Kenzie. "I shall want it myself." "You won't eat that." "I bet I do."

"There ain't many eat their porridge the first time." "I shall eat it. I want that cup of tea, too."

"You better put that porridge round the corner and give it me."

When they came round with the porridge Kenzie found that his companion had been right. He stuck his spoon into the stuff but the crust was so thick and rubbery that the spoon wouldn't penetrate and, in Kenzie's words, "when you took your weight off it, it just come level again. I think if I'd let the spoon go, the force of that skin being like 'larstic, the spoon would've hit the ceiling. I broke into it but couldn't eat it. So when they opened the doors again for us to put our breakfast things outside I just shoved it round the corner to the next cell, and when I looked again it had gone. This feller in the next cell had got it."

The doors remained open. Kenzie again shut his door for privacy's sake and instantly locked himself in. After a long time he heard a whistle blow, followed by a lot of shuffling about. At last the footsteps stopped and the prison became dead silent. No one came for Kenzie. It was too cold to stand around, so he walked up and down and then dragged the chair up to the window to see what was going on. In the distance he saw three green plovers loping in characteristic flight across the sky, and he thought to himself: "How nice to be a bird now." As the minutes passed it got colder and colder. There was snow on the ground outside. When there was still no sound, he wrapped his feet in a blanket and put another round his head and then sat facing the door. He had been in this position about an hour when he heard the heavy footsteps of a warder. The peep-hole shot back and Kenzie saw an eye looking at him.

"What you doing in there?" the screw asked.

"I'm locked in here."

"You ought to be on the parade ground with the others. Who locked you in?"

"I locked myself in."

This plainly beat the warder who fell back on, "Lead on." Kenzie led on. In the yard he found three hundred prisoners exercising in pairs. Kenzie, as a late arrival, was told to walk on his own, but whether this was because the screws thought that they had a dangerous deviationist on their hands or just a prisoner out of the usual run never really became clear. At every stage during those first few days, whether when being ordered to the mailbag shop, or to line up for searching after leaving work, Kenzie's unfamiliarity with prison routine seemed to puzzle the screws almost .as much as it baffled the prisoner. Perhaps they merely expected everyone to have had previous experience.

At the end of six weeks Kenzie was told by his companions in crime that he would shortly "come on stage". This meant that he would receive the regulation three cigarettes and one halfpenny per week. Kenzie was plainly not cut out to be a prison "snout baron" for he protested innocently to his companions, "But I don't smoke." He caught on quickly, however.

"When I did come on stage I couldn't keep the other prisoners out of my cell. I was flogging them little bits of cigarettes, perhaps an inch at a time. I got sugar and bread for the fags, and soon I had more food than I could eat. I even got used to the porridge. I got about three plates for half a cigarette. And I got to like it ver' ver' much."

At the end of the six weeks, too, Kenzie was given work more to his liking than waxing the ends of mailbag thread. He was sent to the prison garden and told to instruct eight Italians in digging. One day he was at work with this party when he heard wings beating high up in the winter haze. Kenzie said to himself, "Swans." It was a moment of intense excitement. He looked up and saw three whoopers heading straight over the prison yard, their pinions making that wonderful and peculiar whistling creak that only a swan in flight can produce.

Kenzie at his easel in 1950.
Photo by courtesy of Don Andrew.

"I was that stirred up I started running about, waving my arms, and whooping back at them. All the other prisoners stopped work. They thought I'd gone crazy."

So did the prison officer. He obviously recognized that Kenzie was a man of peculiarities and was basically harmless, so he said not unkindly: "If anything else flies over you must keep yourself to yourself. Otherwise I'll have to peg you."

As the end of the two months drew near, the pull of the marsh became irresistible. Kenzie begged a slate and pencil from the library to draw ducks and geese. He found a book on birds in the library, too. The fly-leaf of this was temptingly plain and a considerably better surface than that presented by the prison slate. Kenzie borrowed a pen and ink and drew a marshland scene with pinkfeet geese. He was so pleased with the result that he signed his name, and next morning showed it to his neighbour.

"You want to get rid of that as soon as you can," said the man in the next cell. "If they find that in there you'll have to do the other month."

"No!"

"You will. You'll be pegged for destroying prison property." Ke'nzie was so frightened at this prospect that he tore the fly-leaf out, ripped it into small pieces, chewed them until they were unrecognizable and dropped them one at a time into his washing water.

"At last," he recalls, "the big day came. They brought my clothes to the cell. I went before the Governor. They gave me some money to come home and when I got to Boston I had two shaves."

Back in Sutton Bridge the family had a suitable welcome prepared for him. Kenzie's eldest son had been out and poached him a brace of nice French partridges. There they were sizzling in the oven to greet him.

Gaol did not, however, cure Kenzie of poaching. He was not to give the game up—except perhaps for rare raids many miles from his home territory—until the 1950s, when, as will emerge, he turned all his energies onto becoming a professional wildfowl guide. He came out of Lincoln prison in late March 1947. When the season came round again that year, Horry and Kenzie were once more in trouble. This time they had with them a previous accomplice of Kenzie's, Banty Mann.

The Austin Seven was pressed into service for this raid on Mr Caudwell's farm up by Shep White's Cottage at the Holbeach end of the marsh. They had done quite well and were returning merrily. Kenzie had four hares and three partridges in his rucksack under the seat, and there was more game behind the spare wheel.

They had gone a mile on the road when they were stopped by two policemen and Mr Fred Green, a most imposing figure, and Caudwell's head keeper.

The opening was routine. "Now then, Kenzie," said the sergeant, "what do you think you've been up to?"

"Nothing, Sergeant. We've just been after a few duck and that."

"What have you got in your rucksack? You'd better just empty it out."

So Kenzie tipped out the four hares and three partridges on the road, saying to himself as he did so: "Well, that's a good start on a Sunday morning and all."

Horry and Banty denied that they had anything, but the police now knew the secret of the Austin's cubby-hole, The sergeant undid the trap-door and there by the spare wheel were eleven pheasants, some rabbits and a few hares.

The constable said to Kenzie: "I'll have your gun."

"Oh no you won't," said Kenzie, and began to run for it. But he'd picked up the four hares and three partridges and stuffed them back in his bag while the police were searching the car, and these now weighed him down badly, slowing his getaway. The constable soon overtook him and put him down with a flying tackle.

Shades of Lincoln gaol loomed before Kenzie once more.

He lay perfectly still and told the constable: "You needn't worry. I'm quite peaceable. I'm not in a fighting mood."

Kenzie recalls sadly: "We went home without guns, without pheasants, without hares and without rabbits, and three weeks later the summonses came."

The weather was sharpish, so that when the case came up at Holbeach three weeks later, the full evidence, in a good state of preservation, could be laid out on the courtroom floor. There, like a still life, were the three guns, the eleven pheasants, the fifteen hares, the three partridges, and a pile of rabbits.

All three lost their guns. Each was fined £5 for coming from land in possession of game, and £5 for killing game on a Sunday, with 6*s.* costs.

Kenzie's cutting-book contains the headline from the local paper which reported the case:

A SIGHT FOR SORE EYES AT
HOLBEACH MAGISTRATES' COURT

Kenzie's luck was indeed out. About this time he had two unfortunate experiences with swans. These adventures are worth retelling at this point for they perfectly illustrate the formal pattern of defiance, flight, bluff and capitulation which was always evident in his skirmishes with the law.

He had been out after geese at Thorney with Ivan Carlisle, another of his regulars, this time from Wisbech. They had been unlucky, but, as they drove home along French Drove, Kenzie spotted two swans flying low towards the road.

"Step on it," he said, "we'll just about cut them off."

While Carlisle stepped on it, Kenzie loaded his gun in the car.

The swans flew onward on creaking pinions and Carlisle pulled the car to a skidding stop so that Kenzie could leap out and discharge a lethal right and left.

Kenzie picked the birds up and pushed them into the boot of the car. They were mute swans. "Do you want them, Mr Carlisle?"

"No, thanks."

"Good, then I've got a place for them."

It was Christmas time. Back home Kenzie went out to do some Christmas shopping—was it, perhaps, to buy some sage and onions for stuffing? On the way to the shops he passed the British Legion Club and, from the open door, a mate hailed him to play off his Christmas billiards handicap. He was in the middle of a useful break when a policeman came in and asked: "Is there a Mr Mackenzie Thorpe here?"

"That's me," said Kenzie. "Why?"

"Just step outside, please."

The constable explained that they had just received a call from Wisbech complaining that two swans had been shot. The police had stopped a car and found blood and feathers in the back, and the driver had admitted that his companion had been a Mr Mackenzie Thorpe.

"Did you shoot two swans?" asked the constable.

"Certainly," said Kenzie, who realized that Carlisle must have slipped up. "But you can't do nothing about it. They was whoopers."

"Whoopers?"

"Yes, wild swans."

Kenzie knew perfectly well that all swans, whether whoopers, Bewicks or mute swans, were protected, but he was relying on the ignorance of the police. The constable went away gratifyingly baffled. Kenzie left his billiards match and hurried back to his council house in Allenby's Close, and there he hid the swans in the outside lavatory cistern.

Very soon the constable showed up again. "The sergeant says I'm to take possession of those swans."

"You're too late. I've sent them away."

The constable was pretty certain that he was being made a fool of, and he went away very annoyed. Shortly after he had gone, Ivan Carlisle turned up to apologize. "I can't think what I was doing. They asked me who was with me and I just let it slip out."

"Well, that ain't the thing," said Kenzie. "Not the thing at all."

"Where are the swans now?"

Kenzie showed him the cistern. They were still laughing at this ruse when a police car pulled up and the constable came up the path, this time accompanied by his sergeant.

The sergeant took a reasonable line. "Look here, Kenzie, if they were whoopers, were you entitled to shoot them?"

"Of course I were. They're wild."

"How would we tell if they were whoopers?" "Well, for one thing the beaks are different." "Look here, you get the heads back and show me." "Oh, I couldn't do that. It's not possible."

"All right then, Kenzie, we'll have to prosecute and see how we get on."

When the coast was clear Kenzie removed the swans from the cistern and hung them up in an outhouse. Then he went down to the village and 'phoned London. Now this was an exceptional step for a citizen of Sutton Bridge to take, particularly when it is revealed that the number he called was that of a firm of solicitors.

But two things prompted this action. First, that Kenzie was now really worried, and second that these were exceptional solicitors. One of the partners was a wildfowling client of his.

Kenzie explained his problem.

The wildfowling solicitor's reaction was to the point, even if his language was not particularly professional. "You," he said, "are a silly clot. To start with there's a penalty for shooting *any* swan, but it looks to me, Kenzie, as though you've out-smarted yourself this time. You've gone and shot two mute swans, for which you can be fined five pounds apiece, but you've told the police that you've knocked off a pair of whoopers, and they come a bit more expensive. In fact, you can be fined twenty-seven pounds ten for each of them. You could even be sent to gaol. About all you can do is to say you made a mistake and produce the corpses to prove it."

Kenzie rang off. He confesses that the mention of gaol—for this occurred after his visit to Lincoln—had left him shaking at the knees. Next day he took the swans out to Wisbech and threw them in a drain. He wasn't going to show himself up as a man who didn't know a mute from a whooper.

In due course the summonses came, and the police "saw how they got on". From their point of view the matter went satisfactorily. Kenzie was fined £25 with £2. 18*s*. 6*d*. costs.

The second swan misadventure demonstrates exactly the point to which Kenzie was willing to push actual physical defiance in a set-to with the law.

He had gone with a young, though inexperienced, shot, Brian Reece, to bag some swans at Peterborough sewage farm, not far from Whittlesey. Reece had provided the transport—a motorbike and side-car. There were sixty swans on the filter beds, and, at the first drive, Reece walked them to Kenzie. Three birds fell dead to a right and left and a quick re-load. Kenzie put his three swans in a sack and hid them by the motor-bike. Reece then demanded to have a go, and Kenzie agreed to walk the swans over him.

However, Reece was nothing like such a good shot and his two barrels killed one swan far out of reach on the flooded filter bed and crippled the other, which glided down, wounded, into the sewage farm.

Reece was keen on retrieving one at least of these birds and so, unknown to Kenzie, he walked three-quarters of a mile to the sewage farm manager's house and asked a woman there how deep the water was.

"Why?" she wanted to know.

"Because I've shot some swans," he explained.

The woman shut the door and disappeared inside smartly, no doubt to tell her husband.

Reece walked back and joined Kenzie, who gave it as his opinion that it was high time that they had something to eat. So they sat down on the bank of a filter bed and opened up their sandwiches. While they were having lunch in this salubrious setting, Kenzie spied a small car pulling up outside the sewage farm building. He put his glasses on it and saw one man in plain clothes step out. This did not particularly worry him. Nevertheless, he thought that it would be wise to move very shortly and suggested they pack up directly they had eaten. They had started away on the bike with the three swans in the sack, when Kenzie looked round to see the car following them. The car came close up behind them and hooted, and the driver signalled them to stop. Reece pulled up and together they waited, fearing the worst. The worst was confirmed not so much by the face of the man in the mackintosh who climbed out of the car as by the size of his feet. They could only belong, as it turned out they did, to a policeman.

"I've had a complaint you've been shooting swans," were the opening words.

Kenzie said: "You can't do nothing about them. They was shot on the river and flew into the sewage farm."

"I can't help that. I'll have to take your guns and ammunition."

"You can't do that neither," said Kenzie. "If we was coming from land in possession of game you could take our guns, but swans is wildfowl."

At that moment reinforcements arrived for the law in the form of a constable who already—and few didn't—knew Kenzie.

"Now then, Kenzie," said the new arrival, "what have you been up to?"

Kenzie explained.

"Well," said the second constable, "you'd best come up to the station and explain there."

Brian Reece's gun was already in a canvas case. As a general precaution Kenzie now put his own gun in with it. He did not know quite why he did this. He just had an instinctive feeling that one bundle might be easier to handle than two.

Outside the police station there was a moment or two of confusion while constables and their captures disembarked. Kenzie seized on this to grab the two guns in their single case and hide them in an outbuilding of a nearby house.

In the station the sergeant on duty acted very sternly. He expressed surprise that Kenzie and Reece should have done such a thing as to shoot a beautiful bird like a swan and demanded the guns.

"You can't have those," said Kenzie again. "Anyway, I've put them on a lorry and sent them home to Sutton Bridge."

"Are you trying to beat the law, Thorpe?"

"Oh no sir, it's just that you've got no right to have those two guns."

"Haven't I? Well, I don't know about that exactly, but I'm going to make a case out of this if I can."

"Well, that's up to you, sir."

All particulars were taken and then Kenzie and Reece were allowed to go.

Outside in the street Reece was showing the strain. "I must go to the lavatory," he said.

"All right, you go. And I'll just pick up these here two guns and then we'll be away. I'll meet you at the top of the street."

Kenzie collected the guns from the outhouse, but he hadn't gone far up the street with them when he heard feet pounding along and a police whistle blowing. Behind him, in full cry, was one of the constables who had apprehended him on the sewage farm. Kenzie ran for it. An old man stepped out in Kenzie's path. "Stop him!" shouted the constable, blowing the whistle. "Stop him!" The old man took one look at Kenzie's purposeful figure and quickly jumped back inside the doorway he had just left. But now bad luck stepped in and tripped Kenzie up. The strap on the guncase broke and the two weapons fell to the pavement. While he was picking them up the officer tackled him.

Kenzie saw that the game was up. "All right," he said, "I know what you want. Here are the guns. But you can't keep them."

Back at the station Kenzie faced the sergeant again who said :

"That's twice today you've made a fool of my constable. You can keep the guns, but now I'm going to prosecute as hard as I can for those swans."

Kenzie and Reece retained their guns and also the three swans, which the police never found, but they were summoned and duly appeared at Whittlesey magistrates' court.

The beak wanted to know why Kenzie should wish to shoot a swan.

"For food, sir," said Kenzie. "Why, during the war I shot two hundred and fifty on them."

"Well, they're protected nowadays."

Kenzie felt that the service he was doing in providing food was not being fully appreciated. Later in the case it transpired that a hand at the sewage farm, who was called as a witness, had eaten the swan left dead by Reece.

"What did they eat like?" Kenzie wanted to know.

"Very good eating. In fact, a beautiful dish," admitted the witness.

"In that case," said Kenzie, "I'm very pleased to hear it."

The magistrate took a different view of the service Kenzie was doing the public. Kenzie and Reece were each fined £5 for killing swans and £4 for wounding.

6

Poaching is, of course, theft, though it is a form of theft hard to define, for are not pheasants and hares free to come and go, to fly or run from one man's land to another as weather conditions and food supplies suggest to them? Can anyone, therefore, be said to own a pheasant? The law sidesteps this by describing daytime poaching offences as "trespass in pursuit of game" or "corning from land in pursuit of game". The illegal night shooter or netter the law names outright as a "night poacher", for the cover of darkness makes the offence more dastardly and precise in every possible way.

However you describe his offence the intention of the poacher remains the same: to take something which, temporarily perhaps, is another man's property. He may do it for sport as much as gain, but, give or take a split hair or two, it is stealing. A certain romanticism surrounds the lone poacher in the town-dweller's eye, brought up as he is on the Archers of Ambridge. It is doubtful whether the gamekeeper sees the single-handed expert in quite this light, but he certainly would go so far as to put him a cut above the city slickers who rob his coverts with .22 rifles and then make their escape in cars. At least the keeper has a chance of keeping his eye on the local expert, and, in the last analysis, the rural poacher is the same sort of chap as himself. This isn't to say that he makes a romantic figure of him. He is simply the lesser of two evils. To the gamekeeper the local poacher is still a thief, and a thief who is undoing the keeper's own hard work, but one he understands.

Even when seeing Kenzie Thorpe's operations in their true and legalistic light, and pleasing yourself whether you enhance them with any of the romantic folk-lore glow that surrounds country characters, one thing cannot be denied. Kenzie is an original, and a type of original that is fast vanishing from the countryside. A handful of men up and down the land, just like himself—and they are mainly keepers or poachers—know things about the countryside which, unless wrested from them and preserved, are likely soon to be forgotten altogether. What follows in this chapter, then, is a hard kernel of knowledge concerning the sheer technique of East Anglian poaching, given in Kenzie Thorpe's own words.

Preparation: "You've got to be as cunning as a fox to outwit the keepers, the farmers, the agricultural labourers, the inmates of the cottages, and everyone who lives around your poaching area. You've got to keep your eyes and ears open. Notice any little sound or sight you've never heard or seen before. You've got to know your ground, your ditches, your roadways on which a car can approach in the evening without its headlights. You've got to know every tree, every bush, every haystack. If there's a new object sticking up from a dyke or bank you must investigate it before you start work. If you don't, you'll be nervous and this will put you off. At night don't think of starting until every light's gone out and everything's gone still.

"Outwitting a gamekeeper can be very simple if you stick to the rules. You've got to know his whereabouts and his movements, his habits and the company he keeps. Does he visit pubs? Does he have regular cronies? If he has, then, with a bit of luck, you've got him, for you know where he'll be at certain times.

"Stay clear of the estates with several keepers because there they can run a duty roster, like in the Army, and keep guard four on, four off. Keep an eye on the keeper's cottage when you're out at night. In the war, the blackout sometimes beat us. You couldn't see when the keeper had got out of bed to find out what that shot he just heard was all about. But after the war it was different. He had to put his lights on to get dressed.

"And when you're out in the fields at night, have a shot here and a shot there with a four-hundred-and-ten-bore gun. That way they'll never catch up with you. Once you're on the job, keep to the fields and dykes and never cross a road. Never go near a cottage for, no matter if you're walking like a cat, some dog will give you away with his yap-yap...

"No matter how successful you've been, never visit the same place two nights running. If they know the place has been poached they'll be watching for poachers again, but they won't catch you if you're working five miles away on a different farm."

Torching: "One of my favourite ways of operating at night has been to take the roosting pheasants out of trees with a .22 rifle. You fix the torch underneath. You try to spot the birds without using the light. Sometimes there are as many as ten in one tree. If there's a good wind blowing and the night is rough you can sometimes get every one of these pheasants without any trouble at all. The method is this: first show your torch on the ground. You look up and find your first bird with the naked eye. Straightaway cock your torch onto the first bird and shoot. Leave the dead bird where it falls. You drop your torch again and switch off. Pick your next bird by naked eye, then up with the rifle and repeat the performance. Don't move between shots. Stand dead still and the birds won't take fright. I've had, in one tree, nine cocks out of nine, never picking the birds up until I'd knocked them all down.

"When I dursen't use a torch for any reason I'd go round the trees with a four-hundred-and-ten-bore gun. This allows you to be just that much more inaccurate. I use short cartridges loaded with number six shot. You aim by running your gun up the tree and firing directly the barrel blots out the bird."

Torching on grass: "You can use the .22 rifle with the torch on short grass and short clover and ploughed land, also stubble, providing the stubble hasn't got long clover on it, when you can't see your birds. Short grass fields are the best where bullocks have been feeding, but look out if the bullocks are still there because they make so much commotion that the pheasants won't jug [roost] there. The best field is one off which the bullocks have been taken for about a fortnight...

"You want severe weather for this sport: snow, rainstorms, or gales are ideal. Whatever the weather you must walk head-wind. You use your torch on the bottom of the rifle and you sweep the torch very slowly from left to right, about ten degrees either side of your line of approach. You must walk very, very slowly, too. You never pass a bird. Pick the right night and they'll sit very, very close. You can walk within five yards of them. Sometimes you'll have four or five pheasants jugging all round you. You can knock out your first bird, and then put the torch on the next. I've had as many as five or six without moving a step. If you don't kill your birds dead, any fluttering will put up the rest of the pheasants around you. But they won't fly far at night and they'll settle in the same field. You can attend to them later. If you do the job thoroughly it will take you about three hours to work out a forty-acre field. I can remember one night with Horry going on a fifty-acre grass field at twelve midnight and coming off at three a.m., using two torches. Horry was walking five yards away on my left. He covered the ground ten degrees to the left of our line, and I was shooting ten degrees to the right. As usual Horry was too talkative and I said to him: 'When you see one don't say to me Look up here's a pheasant. Just give a low whistle.' The first pheasant Horry saw he got so excited he shouted: 'Look up, old chap, here's one. Look, look,' and I hissed at him: 'Don't make a damn' noise like that, just give a low whistle.' But the old cock didn't hear there was that much wind blowing so I just swung round and panned him out. We took thirty-seven pheasants off that field that night."

Torching hares: "There are about four ways of working a torch on the ground. Pheasants you torch with your beam no more than fifteen yards away from you. You torch about the same for partridges, but hares are different. You need to be fifty or sixty yards in front of you and you want a torch with five battery cells giving a beam of five hundred feet. Mine will nearly burn a hole in a cottage wall. Whenever you pick up a hare you take the torch off the hare and then swing it back to her. You'll see her still sitting there, but if you keep the beam on you'll find she'll run immediately. And if she runs you'll never keep the light on her and she'll put up a lot more hares and also pheasants as she jinks past them on the ground. You must learn to keep the jobs separate. If you're torching pheasants, then torch pheasants. If you're torching hares then go for hares. But don't try to do both or you'll never get good results. If the weather is rough you'll have a better chance with hares, just as you will with the birds. In a gale of wind you can get within a yard of a hare, quite easily."

Calling hares: "This is another way of making a good bag. In the early spring of the year I've stood in the middle of a field of grass in pitch darkness and called hares all around me. I've knocked over seven or eight in five minutes. You call the hares across the field and then put the torch on them and, believe me, you can get them as easy as pie when you know how.

"When the moon is full in February and March and sometimes as late as April I call a lot of hares. You go in a dyke with a twelve-bore gun. Young wheat is the best land to start calling over. Sometimes they'll come too fast. You get a right and a left and load up again and before you've closed the gun there are another two. I've had eighteen hares from one dyke, calling over one field, in one and a half hours. What they come to the call for I really can't imagine, unless it has something to do with their mating sounds. I've never heard a hare call unless wounded, and then it's not the same noise. The call brings hares of all sorts, not only bucks, but does carrying young, does in milk, rabbits sometimes, and if you're calling just as the sun goes down you can expect to see a few partridges turn up first. The noise is a bit like the sound you get when you blow on a piece of grass between your cupped hands, only not so high. Again it's a bit like a dog yelping, only flatter. You repeat it over and over, with the sound rising all the time. I get it by blowing, close, on the back of my hand."

Torching other birds: "It's amazing what you can do with the torch. I remember being on a piece of cut clover one wild night. It was about two a.m. when my torch picked up eight pinkfoot geese in the clover with their heads up, looking towards the light. I could shoot one with the rifle, but no more. So I decided to catch one with my hands for my collection. I walked nice and steady right up to the geese and seized one by the neck. When I put it in my sack it lay quiet. They do, you know. Mind you, the night I caught that goose it wasn't fit for a dog or a beast to be out at all.

"In my twenty years of torching I've picked up little grebe, mute swan and pinkfoot geese. I've caught common gull in midair flying across the sands at night. I've torched knot on the sands and browned into them and got as many as forty at a shot. I've picked pheasants, rabbits, partridges, and hares up at night by hand. Golden plover, grey and green plover—I've picked them up; whimbrel and curlew also. But, as I say, it's got to be an *extrastrordinary* night. It's got to be rough, and I do mean rough. The best nights of all are when the winds are that strong that the telephone wires are slipping off the poles and great boughs are breaking off the trees.

"If you want to go poaching, pick a Sunday night. The reason is that the farmers, the gamekeepers and all the farm labourers have got to go to work on Monday and so they have an early night."

Nerve: "I hear a lot about poaching. People are always bragging about knocking off the odd pheasant or the odd hare and I often think to myself: 'You ought to be out with me sometimes.' I remember walking four or five miles with the .22 rifle to a certain farm I had my eye on one rough Sunday night, but when I got there they had a party on. Four or five big cars on the drive and the lights on at twelve at night. They was enjoying theirselves and there was me shivering under the trees, with the pheasants all above my head waiting to be shot. And I dursen't shoot them with this party there because they might see the torch from the house. I stood there for a couple of hours and then all of a sudden the door opens and they start coming out. And you can hear them talking to one another.

" 'Good night. I'll see you tomorrow.'

" 'Good night. Don't forget to ring me on the 'phone.'

"A lot of silly women all promising to meet each other in King's Lynn for coffee on Monday, though I can't think what the hell there is left to talk about, and I say to myself: 'I wish to God you'd get out on it and go, and not stand there gabbin'. Go on-get out on it.'

"I've watched the party go and I've seen the farmer and his wife go upstairs, and within quarter of an hour the light go out. Half an hour later I've been round the garden taking the pheasants off the trees.

WILDFOWL BY MACKENZIE THORPE

Mallard

Pink Foot

Teal Drake

Pink Foot

Snow-Goose

Mallard Duck

Red-breasted Goose

Wigeon Drake

"You never quite get used to starting in on a situation like that. Your tummy's full of butterflies and your heart starts thumping, but you soon get acclimatized once you've had a shot or two. You're soon shooting right against the house-the .22 with short cartridges doesn't make no more than a spit-and you're dropping the birds on the front lawn and on the gravel drive.

"I can remember one place in particular. Horry and I went there one night to do the job at pheasants. A beautiful rough night. The first two trees were nearly on the front lawn of the house. There were two cocks up the first tree. I shot the first cock and got him in the rear and he flew towards the house and went straight through one of the downstairs windows. I never saw anything like it in all my life. Horry said: 'Come on, let's get out of here.' I said: 'Go on. That wasn't the bedroom window. We'll get them other ones.' And I just cocked up the old gun and got the other one and we took seven more besides. We had a lovely night, but what-ho in the morning when the farmer woke up and found a pheasant in the house, dead, shot with a .22 rifle!"

Not all Kenzie's poaching was done with a gun. Any form of poaching appealed to him. Netting with its need for planning, silence and secrecy once had a strong hold on him. He did a great deal of trail-netting with Horry Savage in the early days of their partnership but gave it up eventually for reasons that he makes clear. Here is Kenzie on trail-netting:

"Trail-netting is done for pheasants and partridges on stubble and clover fields at night. The net itself is fourteen yards long by thirteen feet deep. You have two poles at each side of the net, thirteen foot each pole. The net has a top and bottom line reaching between poles, and a middle line as well. The best nets are made of four-inch diamond mesh, or better still four-inch square. Pheasants, particularly, don't get tangled quite so much in square mesh. The net is carried by two men at about ten degrees to the ground. The right-hand man carries his pole left hand forward, right hand down. The left-hand operator has right hand forward, left hand down. You get your net laid out on the stubble in the dark, then you pick it up and stand still. The right-hand man takes charge. He gives one twitch of the net when he's ready to start. You may go a long while before you get a tap but you can feel the pheasant jump as soon as the net touches it. You drop the net immediately. You run to the front of the net and your mate runs to the back. You take the pheasant out, wring its neck, and put it in the bag, pick up, twitch the net to start and away you go again. When you get to the end of the field, you give one pull on the pole and that makes your mate stop immediately. Then you give two more pulls and he wheels round ready to start off back up the field again. You carry on until you've covered the whole field.

"One night on a clover field with Horry a thick haze came over. It was very frosty and you could see your tracks so you could keep nice straight paths up and down the field. We was catching pheasants galore. The pheasants were that worried by the mist they wouldn't get up. Some of them were letting the net go right over them. One particular time when we dropped the net we took the pheasants out and Horry took a step forward and put his foot on another cock just sitting on the stubble and we caught that one as well. The pheasants was getting up and going down in the same field. They was properly skeered that night and we was properly skeered too because we were catching so many. We took forty-three pheasants and four partridges that night, and we'd only done a quarter of the field.

"Of course the gamekeepers get very crafty. They bush the fields with posts and sticks and thorn branches so that the net gets caught up, and then you've had it.

"I can remember one night when Horry, Banty Mann and I wanted to go after pheasants with the trail-net. I suggested that we take the net, but also a twelve-bore shot-gun with a torch on. We made arrangements with a fellow called Dick Garner to take us down in his car and drop us at a big barn, and then come back for us next morning at eight o'clock. We set off in the car about half past ten at night and arrived on the job about eleven. We walked across the fields to a dyke where our poles were hid in a tunnel. I told Banty and Horry to do the same field Horry and I had got the forty-three on. I made sure that they knew how to put the net together, then I went off with the gun to look for rabbits and hares. It was a lovely night, blowing and rainy, and it wasn't long before I was among the rabbits. I come to a warren and shot four and went across the dyke onto a stubble field, and no sooner had I crossed than I switched the torch on and there to my surprise sat three pheasants, all cock birds. I drew back at about twenty yards, went down on one knee to try to get the lot, and shot.

But I only got two. I picked them up and torched the field for half an hour but couldn't find another bird. I returned to the warren and got a left and right at rabbits running back to their burrows, but the second shot blew the bulb of the torch. I hadn't got a spare. So I turned back to a pea-stack where we were to meet, and where we had hid some bread and cheese and some bottles of beer. I waited three-quarters of an hour for the netters to return, then I went to look for them. I couldn't hear anybody. I didn't make any noise in case they thought it was someone after them and dropped the net and run away. In the dark they might never find the net again. No luck, so I went back to the pea-stack, had a meal and soon I thought to myself I'll go and look round the trees. I went to a little place called Acre Farm on Caudwell's estate and as soon as I got there I saw a feast of pheasants just sitting up in the trees. I counted forty all told. I returned back because I left the gun in the stack. As I set out again I could hear my mates slushing down a dirt roadway. As soon as they came near I called out: How many you got? How ever many you got?

We ain't got none, they said. Whyever not? I said. 'Cos there's been bullocks on that field, they said, and the bullocks' hoofmarks are all full of water. Well, I said, you don't expect pheasants to roost in the wet, do you? No, they said, we don't, but wherever do you think they've got to? I know where they've got to, I said. They're all sitting up in the trees. What trees? Horry said. All round Caudwell's, I said. Well, Horry said, you can't do nothing about that. Can't I, I said. I'm going to give 'em one with the old twelve-bore. It'll make a hell of a lot of noise, Horry said. Well, I can't help that, I said. If you can pick 'em up as fast as I can shoot 'em you'll be all right. Come on, shove them poles into that tunnel and let's get going. So away we went.

"We walked through the yard and there right against the house I saw the first two. Bang, bang. Down they come, and I was shooting that many my mates had to shout to me to stop because they couldn't pick them up. We only done half the trees and we got sixteen pheasants. We got away across the dyke, and I was the last one over, and I was carrying half a dozen pheasants and four or five rabbits and I missed my jump and hit my foot on the bank and burst my boot in half right across the instep. Well, we got to the bank and sorted the birds out. \ Ale walked along the road and then we heard someone coming behind us. I looked round at Horry and said to him to look out, someone was after us. So we ran as hard as we could for about a hundred yards and then we realized Banty wasn't with us. Then we heard him hollering. We'd lost him in the darkness and it was him after us trying to catch up. I said to him: 'Banty, man, don't you dare do that again. You well nigh frit me dead. I thought we were going to have to drop this load of pheasants.'

"By and by I had to stop to cut the front part of my boot off which was flapping about something terrible. Well, we got to the pea-stack at last where Dick Garner was supposed to meet us with the car. Horry and Banty climbed into the stack and went to sleep behind a pile of sugar beet. So, as it was breaking day, I went down the hedge and shot another six pheasants. They didn't hear me shooting but when I got back I woke them up. They looked at the pheasants. Wherever did you get them? they wanted to know. As I stood talking, another old cock flew across this roadway and into a piece of mustard. So I left them and walked up the dyke towards the foreman's house and put the old cock up and shot it. By and by the foreman come along in his car and said: Didn't I just see you shoot a pheasant, Kenzie? No, I said, you just seen me shoot a pigeon. Oh, he said, I could have sworn that was a pheasant. But I had a pigeon on top of the bag I'd shot the previous night, but luckily he didn't feel it, for it was stiff and cold.

"When he'd gone I got the others and told 'em we'd better get away from the place if we didn't want to get caught. We walked three and a half miles along the road, me with me toes out of me boot, before Dick Garner came and picked us up, and all he could say was that he had overlaid. We might easily have been caught with all that stuff on us. We had twenty-five pheasants and eight rabbits, and the fines would have been pretty heavy. And that's what you get for not working properly together.

"We packed up trail-netting in the end. Hiding the poles was the trouble. Once we hid them in a tunnel and the floods came up and floated them out and they were found. Another time we hid them in a wheat-straw stack and we went by there one day and they'd started stripping the stack and we saw the poles lying out on the ground. So we lost that lot. A third set we put in a strawstack that went on fire. So we packed up. It was a very exciting business, trail-netting, but we liked to feel free and not have to worry about finding our gear."

Flight-netting: "This used to be a lifetime's study. I say 'used to be' because now it's illegal. You need a pitch dark night. You use a net eighteen yards long and six feet deep. The nets were set out in threes. For this you need four nine-foot poles for each net. You stick the poles into the mud with eight feet showing. The nets are threaded through top and bottom lines, and you set them so that they are only four feet deep with two feet lost in the belly. You want this loose net to trap the bird when it hits them in the darkness. Most flight-netters made their own nets of diamond mesh six inches by six. The cotton has to be thin so that the birds can't see it. At a hundred yards in daylight you oughtn't to be able to see the netting, only the poles. Of course you have to set guy ropes to each pole to hold them steady. The skill comes in estimating the tide and deciding where to place the nets, for the high water should just clip the bottom line. Of course, you have to know where the best flight-lines will be. Sometimes the old flight-netters from Drove End way used to have thirty or forty nets out and that was a whole day's work to bundle them up and move them.

"The nets will catch any bird that flies low across the saltings, not only waders but also ducks and geese. I remember one morning catching thirteen brent geese in one net, and believe me, they took some getting out, too. That used to be the art of catching birds in flight-nets though the Wild Birds Protection Act of 1954 stopped it all. Many of the birds I sent to Peter Scott in 1947 for the Wildfowl Trust at Slimbridge were caught in flight-nets."

Honesty and poaching: "I'm not saying I've been a saint, but the one thing that I've never done is to rob anyone of any money. I've seen a gentleman fowler drop twenty-five one-pound notes out of his pocket in the snow that I could have let lay there easily and come back for after flight, but that's not in my game. I'd rob farmers of pheasants. I'd take them under their noses, and partridges and hares. In fact, if I wanted a pheasant that badly and a gamekeeper had one on his plate, I'd sneak into his house and take it, but to take money—I'd never do that.

"I have to admit that sometimes, afterwards, especially when I'd been caught, I felt ver' ver' ashamed of poaching. But I'd soon forget it when I got a gun in my hands again and a pocketful of cartridges and was out amongst the pheasants. It wasn't the money I made from it.

All told, I paid out £150 in poaching fines, and I lost four good guns. Apart from that, I used to give quite a few of the hares and stuff away. I'm not denying, mind, that I made quite a bit from my birds as well. But it wasn't the money at all. It was the sheer thrill of it. And I know if I had my time over again I wouldn't do any different, except that I'd be more cunning about it, and I wouldn't go walking up a man's birds on a Sunday morning, which I used to do for the pure deering of it. I'd be a lot more cunning."

7

SO FAR THIS book has been almost entirely about Kenzie Thorpe's poaching activities. The reader could be pardoned for imagining that poaching was his only and full-time pursuit. True, he worked for Peter Scott. Here and there have been glimpses of other jobs, mainly in wartime, and it must be added that Kenzie has always filled in the off-season months with agricultural work, a taste for which he has probably inherited from his father.

In his autobiography *The Eye of the Wind*, Peter Scott has described Kenzie as an "inveterate poacher". (Indeed, rather surprisingly, it is almost the only reference to his early assistant in the entire 680 pages.) But if Kenzie turned a dishonest penny by selling pheasants and hares, he earned, even in the early days, quite as many honest ones by wildfowling and guiding other guns on the marshes. He declares that he turned professional wildfowler in 1928, by which he means that he first started taking guns out after ducks and geese for a fee in that year. Today, the poaching days—at least within a radius of twenty miles from Sutton Bridge—are over. He is recognized as the leading authority on the habits of ducks and geese along the Lincolnshire shores of the Wash, and gunners come from all over the British Isles to shoot with him. In the past ten years his wildfowling has truly become full-time and professional and his diary is full from October to February with bookings from wildfowlers, many of whom come back season after season.

If Kenzie has amassed an unrivalled store of poaching knowhow, he has equally certainly a unique knowledge of wildfowling. He has collected this over the years in heaven knows how many icebound dawns and sunsets, and often in some very odd company, for wildfowlers as a race are more than a shade eccentric. If the reader is not himself a wildfowler then some setting of the scene is, perhaps, necessary.

The grey geese come to the Wash in October from Iceland and Spitsbergen. Mostly they are pinkfeet, but with some whitefronts and occasionally bean geese thrown in. There are, perhaps, 10,000 of them in a good year. The geese like the Wash because it provides them with two essentials of life: somewhere to feed free from danger, and somewhere to roost free from disturbance. They feed on the vast Lincolnshire fields, often potato fields, and they invariably choose to alight right in the middle where they are practically unapproachable. They roost on the muds and sands which stretch out towards the shallow North Sea from the point at which the green of the saltings ends. Their usual routine is to flight out to roost on the sands at dusk, and to flight in to the fields at dawn, though bright moonlight can upset this pattern. When they first arrive they are inclined to graze the fields within a mile of the sea wall. But by the time they head north again in March they will have eaten their way twenty or more miles inland. In fact, Kenzie is usually shooting them as far inland as Whittlesey Wash, beyond Wisbech, by early January. The farmers tolerate the geese on some crops but not on others. For example, the geese are welcomed on young winter wheat when it first comes through because they graze it down and this results in a stronger second growth: in some areas sheep are put on young wheat for the same reason. All this is apparent to any moderately observant person. However, to place yourself within forty yards—maximum killing range of a shot-gun—of these geese is something quite different. When leaving the sands for the fields the geese can cross the sea wall at any point they choose along ten miles or more of bank. Inland, there are hundreds of square miles of likely feeding grounds from which they can take their pick. It must be added that because of careless and inexperienced shooting at long range by some of the gunners who visit the Wash, the geese, when crossing the coast, are usually at least two gunshots high.

The ducks along the Wash, as anywhere else, flight at the same times, but in the reverse directions. Duck are night feeders and so they come in from their roosting grounds out at sea at dusk and return to the marsh and the open sea at, or before, dawn. Wind and weather affect them perhaps even more than the geese, and in certain conditions they will stay on the marsh all day. To come to terms with them vast knowledge of their local habits as well as of the intricate topography of the marsh and its creeks is necessary.

Both ducks and geese, as well as wading birds, such as curlew and redshank, lose some of their natural caution when the weather is really intolerable for humans. Snow, fog, and gale are what they like least and, consequently, what the wildfowler likes best. The weather will be seen to play an important part in many of the wildfowling experiences about to be related.

One other scene needs to be established before leaving for the marsh-the early morning start of any expedition at Kenzie Thorpe's house, a ritual which certainly hasn't changed since the days when James Robertson Justice came roaring round the corner in his ancient car.

The party is ordered to report at around five-thirty. There are usually two, sometimes three, rarely four fowlers. Often they have stayed the night at the Bridge Hotel. There is a light in the kitchen when they draw up in their cars. This morning they are a little early. They tiptoe round the back in their waders and knock on the kitchen door. Kenzie pokes his head out. He has a muddy white sweater on, and a once-white "Ballyhava" perched on his head like a lunatic night cap. He looks at them disapprovingly. "I thought I told you," he says, "to be here at five-thirty. It's quarter past. I like my fowlers here on time." Discipline must be instilled at the outset. He opens the door a little wider. "Oh well, come in then. The tea's not brewed yet." But the kettle is soon steaming and while the tea, thick brown army style, is drunk, Kenzie briefs his troops. "I hope you've got plenty of cartridges. I'm going to take you down onto the Terrington Marsh. We'll have a go from the sea wall at the morning flight of mallard, and then, if this wind holds, and with the tide dropping we'll move down into the stalk edges and we should be able to shoot pretty strong all the morning. Right now. Let's get going."

The entire party squeezes into one of the cars. The headlights stab out showing a driving, sleety rain slanting horizontally across the road. "Lovely," says Kenzie. "I don't fancy the look of that rain much," says one gun: it is his first visit. "Don't you?" says Kenzie, who sees weather like this, or worse, every morning for at least half the season. The car whips up a cloud of spray as it clears the swing bridge over the Nene and heads down the long straight road towards Terrington. Almost immediately over the bridge the road runs along the top of a high bank and the cross wind here veers the car half-way across the road. "Lovely wind," says the driver, who means it.

Twenty minutes later the party is disembarking by a hayrick in a freezing, sodden, howling darkness. This is the moment when the most hardened case wonders why he has come. "Follow me," says Kenzie. He is already away at a fast lope along the sheltered side of a dyke. He makes remarkable speed, considering the mushy state of the field. A faint hint of false dawn is appearing in the east and there is a good half-mile of this going to the sea wall where the first stand is to be made for a flight that may not materialize, or may pass just out of shot to left or right, or even above, though that is less likely in this kind of weather. The visiting fowlers, who are paying Kenzie £1 per flight for this strange kind of pleasure, soon find themselves uncomfortably hot and know with certainty that once they start standing about they will soon feel equally, if not more, uncomfortably cold. Kenzie forges further ahead. "Keep up!" he hisses. "Keep up!" If the party's what Kenzie calls "the proper sort" it will keep up, more or less: anyway, it won't grumble. But it takes all sorts to fill a professional wildfowler's bag, as Kenzie has found from the very beginning of his career as a guide.

One of the first large parties he took out, in 1929, consisted of four guns who arrived in the middle of one of the snowy periods that seemed to be common on the Wash in those pre-war days. Kenzie's recollection of a succession of very cold winters seems to be real rather than a result of telescoped memory. For the record, then, it was so cold in 1928 that ducks' tongues were frozen to their beaks as they fell, shot from the sky, and there were even brent geese that year driven to open water in the Nene outside the Bridge Hotel at Sutton Bridge. The December of 1929 was arctic again. Kenzie recalls stalking geese with his brother Verdon and having to break the ice in the creeks cautiously so that their footfalls would not alarm the birds. The winter of 1930 was remarkably snowbound; '37 saw some powerfully hard frosts. Kenzie recalls that the ice on the marsh was very thick in 1940 and that there was heavy snow in 1942. The winters of 1944 and 1947 produced freeze-ups and in 1954 it snowed for a whole week. The last good freeze-up was in 1959, when Kenzie recalls having to chip holes for the decoy posts in the ground with a hammer and chisel. Since then there has been nothing that a respectable wildfowler could call real weather. Perhaps our climate is shifting, as some maintain. Whatever the truth, in 1929 it was an exceptionally bitter December.

The wind on this particular day was the best possible one for a big shoot at fowl—north-east. Kenzie marshalled his four guns, all of whom were new to him, and ordered them to put on white clothing. He led them out in the pre-dawn murk and strung them out along what experience told him would be the flight-line on such a morning, with instructions to keep hidden in the creeks allotted to them. He was no sooner in his own position than the wigeon started to come in over him. The birds wanted to pitch in a pool close by him, so he let them whistle over with the wind in their tails, certain that they would bank and come back head to wind for a landing. He heard a spatter of shots from his party at the outset of the engagement, but as the snow piled on heavier and heavier there was no sound. Kenzie continued to shoot until he noticed the tide creeping up the creek at his feet and saw that the moment had come to get off the marsh. This moment of withdrawal can only be judged on any marsh by someone who knows it intimately, for, though the creek in which you are standing may seem to be only just starting to fill, there are invariably other gutters in the rear of you, at a lower level, that fill first and cut you off.

Kenzie went back to collect his guns and shepherd them off.

But the first creek was empty, and so were the hiding-places in which he had placed the others. He began to get worried, for the tide was now making fast and in the murk of the morning someone unfamiliar with the marshes could easily get lost and even wander out to sea. He started to cast around like an old gun-dog for a scent and at last came upon a half-obliterated track in the snow. The footmarks led back towards the sea wall.

He followed the footprints and was reasonably certain that the four men had eventually joined up and gone off the marsh of their own accord, in strict defiance of instructions.

But there were no gunners waiting on the sea wall, and the car had been left a good two miles further inland on a farm track. He slogged along on the now fairly fresh tracks, cursing hard to himself. But when he reached the point at which they had all climbed out of the car some hours earlier there were only the tyre marks to be seen, and these drove away in the direction of Sutton Bridge, some three and a half miles distant. Kenzie had eighteen dead ducks of his own, weighing over two pounds apiece. There was nothing for it but to start out walking through the thick snow to Sutton Bridge. When he reached the Bridge Hotel he burst straight into the dining-room looking like the wrath of God. The four fowlers were sitting down, pink from bath and shave, at the remains of a handsome breakfast.

Kenzie's opening remark was typical: "Well, whatever happened to you then?"

One of the men said: "We were so cold that we couldn't hit a thing. We could hear you blazing off, so we left you to enjoy yourself."

"Did you?" said Kenzie incredulously. "Well, that ain't the thing."

"We thought we were doing you a good turn."

"Did you? Well, the tide was making and you left me to look for you. If I hadn't known the marsh I might have been drowned trying to find you lot."

"Don't worry," said one of the party. "You'll get your money all the same."

"That ain't the thing," Kenzie said again. He was genuinely shocked at infamy on such a scale.

"What time do you want us out tomorrow morning?"

"I'm not sure if I want you out at all, but, seeing as how you've asked, you'd better turn up at four-thirty. And I don't want this to happen again."

"Five-thirty," recalls Kenzie, "was plenty early enough, but I took 'em over some rough stuff that morning, I can tell you, and they behaved theirselves not too bad, considering."

The four guns he found on his hands in January the following season were also green as samphire, but they at least were sportsmen. It was blowing a gale again, and there was thick snow all over the marshes.

"I could see they was very highly strung directly I clapped eyes on them. Very excited they were, and it was their first trip out with me. I could see by their actions they was an exciting crowd so I gave them a bit of a talking-to. 'Now it's snowing hard,' I said, 'so whatever you do don't get any snow down your barrels. Keep your cartridges dry or they'll swell up and jam your guns, and don't go sticking your muzzles into the mud.'

"By Jove, it was cold! We got out of the car and we had two miles to walk in a thick blizzard. They was game all right. They didn't complain. It was dark as hell and the snow and ice was piled up in the creeks three and four feet high. The tide had left it in piles like boulders.

"I placed the guns out in creeks and warned them again about keeping their barrels clear. As it broke daylight the wigeon and even brent geese started to come in from the sea. I was shooting pretty strong and I could hear the other three shooting pretty strong too; a regular barrage. By and by I'd shot out of cartridges. I picked up my birds, They filled my rucksack and I had to tie some round my waist with string. I trudged over to the first gun and he'd shot a few too. I told him the tide was making and we'd have to get off smartly. 'I can't close my breech,' he said. 'Never mind about that now,' I said, 'we'll see to that when we get to the sea wall.' So I whistled and waved to the others and we all come off together.

"I'll say this for them: they'd done ver' ver' well. We had a hundred and fifty wigeon, mallard, brent and curlew between us, but what a state they were in! The first chap had his breech open on two swollen cartridges and couldn't get it closed. The next had two loaded cartridges in his gun and couldn't get them out. The third had one empty case stuck in the gun and had been shooting with one barrel, and the last chap had six inches of mud up each spout. If he'd have let drive another round he'd have just about had it––his barrels would have burst. So you can tell what kind of people they were. But I will say this for them: they did what they were told."

At this period four guns seems to have been Kenzie's unlucky number. That same year another party came to him and asked to be taken wigeon shooting. Two of them had recently returned from Africa where, apparently, they had been big-game shooting. One of the party was called Parsons, "a hell of a great fellow, and when he talked to you he had that much voice he'd somehow make you shudder."

Kenzie led them skilfully round the pools where the wigeon were resting in the crab grass and without disturbing a bird. Parsons did his best to stir them up with his shudder-inducing voice, however, for when Kenzie invited him to take cover in a creek bottom he bellowed: "Have I got to get in there?"

"Yes, sir, I'm afraid you have."

"But there's a lot of mud or slosh or whatever you call it down there."

"That's right, sir, but you won't get no shooting otherwise. We ain't after lion, you know, sir."

Kenzie got the big man down into the creek and left him for his own hiding-place, thankful that the birds were still sitting tight. But Parsons's huge voice reached out after him. "I say—come here, fellow. Where is the Wash?"

Good God, thought Kenzie. "You're standing in it!" he hissed back.

"You mean to say I'm standing on the Wash which runs into the North Sea?"

Oh God, thought Kenzie, I wish you were in the North Sea. "Yes," he snarled. "Now pipe down or you'll have every damn' bird on the marsh heading out to the North Sea."

"Well I just couldn't have believed that I was on the Wash," shouted the man from Africa.

When it broke daylight the safari men started blazing away at everything, gulls, shore larks, the lot. Wigeon came over in clouds and pounds of metal went up, but nothing save metal came down. When the daylight was full Kenzie could see the guns standing out of their creeks, on the open marsh, letting loose at everything that flew within two hundred yards.

Kenzie realized that it was hopeless. At the earliest chance he got them together and led them off.

"They couldn't even walk on the mud or do anything at all. I don't know what it can be like in Africa. They kept on falling down and giggling at theirselves. I thought to myself: 'When I get this lot off I'll be ver' ver' pleased.' And do you know, when we got to the sea wall they were that ignorant they thought it was a line of potato clamps?"

A kind of nervous behaviour pattern appears to overtake fowlers gathered in Kenzie's small kitchen for morning flight before dawn on a cold dark winter's day. No matter how many or how few morning flights they have experienced the questions they ask as they sip their hot sweet tea—a specific at all times against shock—are always the same. In order of regularity Kenzie lists them as follows:

"Will the geese be high this morning?"
"Do you think we will get some geese?"
"How many cartridges do you think we shall need?"
"Do you think it's going to rain?"
"Shall I take my oilskins?"
"Are we likely to get sand or mud in our guns?"
"If it's going to rain, perhaps I'd better take my oilskins. Do you think I'll get too hot carrying them?"

Though most of these questions are unanswerable, Kenzie usually tries to soothe and allay doubts and fears. He recognizes that they are a natural ingredient of most amateur wildfowlers' make-up. Only the hard cases are marsh-wise and self-sufficient, and there are comparatively few of these.

Honest ignorance he puts up with. Disobedience of orders and sheer stupidity is not likely to be treated with the careful good manners he reserves for the merely half-daft.

"I remember once," he says, "three chaps coming out with me. Two of them had twelve-bores and the other a sixteen. It was blowing a gale and I led them out to the stalk-edges in the dark and placed them a quarter of a mile apart.

"I'd just got into my own position when I heard a lot of shouting. You can guess what had happened. One chap had a sixteen-bore and twelve-bore cartridges and the other had sixteen-bore cartridges and a twelve-bore gun. They was hollering and bawling that much that in the end I got out of my creek and changed their guns over for them. But that was nothing to what I had to put up with with the Coventry party."

The Coventry party was twenty-five strong and it arrived—perhaps for the first time in the history of wildfowling—in a coach, just as if it was a seaside day trip, or a match-fishing expedition.

Kenzie held an orders group and issued them with a torch apiece and instructions not to shine it more than was absolutely necessary. He told them that he was going to take them far out on the sands in the dark and place them in a long sandy creek. The tide was dead low, and he could line them up for half a mile in this creek so that the geese, when they came off, were bound to give someone a shot or two. It was a grandiose and ridiculous plan since the success and indeed entire pleasure of wildfowling depends on solitariness and concealment.

It was very dark when the bus arrived at the sea wall. The long file of raw recruits found it even darker when they started stumbling across the green of the marsh and it wasn't long before Kenzie heard shouting behind him. He stopped the advance and went back.

Two of the visitors had passed out cold. They had been drinking the night before and had had a shot or two of rum in the bus on the way down from Sutton Bridge. Now the sheer exertion of slogging out over the saltings had overtaken them. Kenzie looked with disapproval at the corpses. He spotted a third Coventry gunner who looked as though he might fall victim to the same sort of battle fatigue at any second and ordered him to stay with the non-walking wounded. The man seemed quite happy to accept the invitation.

"None of them had seen a marsh before, and I should think at that hour, in the pitch darkness, those men wondered whether they had fallen down into Hell. I got the survivors out at last before day broke and lined them out in the creek as best I could. When dawn came, a proper firework display went off. They was shooting at the gulls, but not hitting them, of course. They must of fired hundreds of cartridges and I had to go along the line telling them for God's sake to stop. Naturally the geese all went wide of us, and a damn' good job they did.

"We spent all day on the marsh and those fellers didn't shoot a thing. At evening flight I'd had enough. The tide was right up the marsh, so I placed them on the landward side of the sea wall. The geese came over nicely and I managed to call some in. Thank heavens they come just wide of my party, but there was a doctor hiding behind the sea wall at the end of the line that was nothing to do with us and he shot a goose, the only goose that day.

"I went up to him and said: 'Thanks for shooting that goose, sir.' And he said, 'Thanks for calling it. It's the first goose I've ever shot.'

"Thank God someone got something out of a day like that. And

Kenzie at his houseboat with his hand-painted warning sign.
Photo by courtesy of Mr & Mrs J. T. Amos

that was the last time I ever took on a bus-load of wildfowlers, not that you could call them that."

The worst sort of wildfowler is the man who won't do what he is told. The individualist is a nuisance in any form of organized shooting, but with coastal wildfowling the dangers that arise from disobedience to the man in charge are multiplied by the very setting of the sport. If you don't know the marsh you must stay where you are so that your guide can find you before the tide cuts off your retreat.

Sometimes, however, disobedience took a form that Kenzie could understand even if he couldn't openly condone it. Take the case of the Whittlesey Wash swan.

The Wash lies twenty miles inland from the sea wall, beyond Wisbech. It is a token of Kenzie's reform that he is actually welcomed on the farms that cover Whittlesey Wash even though they are crawling, like most of this part of Lincolnshire, with pheasants and hares. Kenzie takes his gunners there for the geese and duck, for the area is a favourite feeding ground when the pinkfeet have eaten their way inland late in the season. The River Nene runs behind high banks across the Wash and also a connecting drain called Morton's Leam. These, of course, harbour a large population of mallard, wigeon and teal. The Wash also, at times, attracts a concourse of swans, a bird with which Kenzie, as will be recalled, had had some disreputable encounters.

On this occasion he took a party of eight guns to Whittlesey after the duck. The Wash on this trip lived up to its name. Wash, of course, is a widely used term on these flat lands. It is applied to an area of artificial drainage into which water flows in times of heavy rainfall. In the old days the Washes were the haunts of professional punt-gunners who went out in open boats ("shouts") to take a harvest of the wading birds and wildfowl that settled there. It was the protection of the green plover that finally put an end to this inland gunning.

On this occasion, Whittlesey Wash was half covered with water and the swans had been quick to recognize the fact. Kenzie had been in enough trouble over swans by this time, and so he warned his guns that when evening flight time came the swans would probably get up and go with the duck. "Don't touch 'em," he warned. "They're protected birds."

When it fell dark, the teal and wigeon obliged nicely, heading from the Nene to the flooded fields, and there was plenty of shooting. At last Kenzie went out to round up his party. They had quite a nice bag, but the last gun in the line had something all to himself: a swan.

"Whatever did you want to go and shoot that for?" asked Kenzie, who knew perfectly well.

"I couldn't resist it," said the end gun.

Kenzie didn't argue with this logic. He knew its force too well. "Well now, you'd just better pitch it in the Nene."

"Not likely!" said the end gun. "I want that swan."

"All right, then. Put it in my sack. When did you shoot it?"

"Just before it got dark."

"Oh."

When they reached the cars, Kenzie, who was in the last car, stuffed the swan in the boot. They pulled out of the farmyard on a soft mushy road until they came to a little bridge over Morton's Leam, now, in flood conditions, a fast-flowing fen stream. There the cortege stopped. Kenzie, who knew the signs, feared the worst.

"I thought ver' ver' quickly," he recalls. (He had, after all, had plenty of practice.) "So I nipped out of the car—we was last in the convoy of three—pulled the swan out of the boot and slung it in Morton's Leam. I watched the stream take it away, and I sighed a sigh of relief, for who should come along at that moment but three police officers. They'd searched the first two cars and found nothing and now they were going to give us a going-over.

"I was back in the car by this time, so I stuck my head out of the window and made myself known: 'I'm Mr Mackenzie Thorpe from Sutton Bridge, professional wildfowler.'

" 'Oh,' said the copper, 'and what have you been wildfowling?'

"'Just a few of these old duck, wigeon and teal,' I said. " 'You didn't shoot a swan, I suppose,' they said.

" 'Search the car,' I said. And so they did, but they didn't find nothing."

From this experience Kenzie deduces a sad truth.

"It isn't always the police that come after you. They've got too much on their hands elsewhere. It's the other people. It's roadmen, and postmen, labourers, farmers, and the damned foremen. They're the people who report you, though God knows why they do it."

"And I reckon that gentleman who shot the swan was ver' ver' lucky, though, as I told him afterwards, he hadn't no business to go disobeying orders."

The two gentlemen who disobeyed orders on the day of the big East Coast flood were something quite different. They were lucky to find themselves alive.

It was the afternoon of a February Saturday in 1953 when Kenzie led seven guns, including a very skilful American wildfowler, out onto Terrington Marsh. The tide was due to be high at eight o'clock that night. It was blowing such a gale that it took all the party's strength to move out against the wind. By three p.m. Kenzie noted with apprehension that the water was already beginning to shift up the tidal creeks. By rights it shouldn't have started to "make" much before five-thirty. Something very strange was up. He remembers that he licked his top lip and felt the salt on it. As it was getting dusk he heard a roaring, and, looking out to sea, saw a small tidal wave "on top of the ordinary level of the water". He started out at once to round up his party and get them back to the safety of the sea wall. Five of the guns were in position, but two had left their stations and moved off on their own. Kenzie could hear the tide rustling up the marsh at his rear, and he took his five gunners off at the double, cursing the two men who had moved from their hides against orders. He was quite clear in his own mind that his first obligation was to get the majority to safety. "The tide," he remembers, "was rushing up the green behind us as we ran, a thing I've never seen in all my life, nor never want to see again."

He hoped against hope that he would find the two missing gunners at the cars; but they weren't there either.

Kenzie wanted to go back on the marsh and look for them, but the American seized his arm and wouldn't let him go. The party who were now in the lee of the bank tried to climb to the top to look into the gathering darkness for the two men. But, when they reached the crest of the sea wall, the wind blew them back and they had to crawl over the skyline.

Soon after this the tide either broke or outflanked the sea wall and started washing the tyres of the cars standing behind it. Kenzie had just decided to stick the flood out by sitting on top of the bank when, out of the darkness, the two men appeared. They were very badly scared.

Kenzie stood and cursed them from sheer relief with every oath he could lay tongue to. The two gunners never said a word, but got into the cars.

They pulled out at once, but with the floorboards already awash, and made it away to higher ground. When they reached Sutton Bridge, the water was already in the streets. A tide which was supposed to make twenty-four feet had risen to thirty. The rest of the tragic story of that night along the whole East Coast is well known.

Kenzie realized that the flood might bring an exceptional bag next day. But next morning only five of his gunners reported. The two he had cursed had packed their bags the night before and left. "They never paid me, but I didn't mind. I'd given them a piece of my mind and that was all that mattered to me."

As it turned out, the day following the flood was not one of exceptional sport, which was perhaps as well, for the water had taken its toll of wildfowl and sea-birds.

"The marsh was swept clean of everything. There was no grass left on it," recalls Kenzie. "But there were buoys, and the wreckage of RAF observation towers from the bombing range, and everywhere there was dead birds. I remember seeing shags, black and common guillemots, brent geese, shelduck, gulls, storm petrels, and tufted duck. There were even five dead gannets, and if the big tide can have drowned them what chance would those two damn' stupid wildfowlers have had?"

# 8

WILDFOWLING, LIKE MOUNTAINEERING, is a self-selecting sport as far as its followers are concerned. You don't take up climbing unless you are reasonably certain that the mountains have a special call for you. You don't go on climbing unless you can make yourself at home on the mountain. If you can't conquer your vertigo, or dislike of being chilled to the bone and wet to the skin, then you stop before you fall off. It is much the same with coastal wildfowling. You may think that it would be exciting to flight ducks or geese in a winter dawn, but you will quickly discover whether you have a taste for the discomforts that attend the occasion. If you are half-hearted you won't come again. For Kenzie Thorpe, as a professional guide, there are always the one-timers—and we have seen some of these in action in the last chapter. Fortunately, when the chaff has been blown away on a howling north-easter, the hard stuff remains. It is the hard stuff which these days fills his engagement diary. The real hard cases, what Kenzie calls the proper sort of wildfowler, began to sort themselves out early on in his career.

Mr Wright was one of the first. He is dead now, though not, I fancy, of anything contracted on the marsh. Kenzie remembers him as a tough old fellow. But this was back in 1930 when Kenzie was twenty-two, and the fact is that Mr Wright was probably only about fifty-five. Wright was a bank manager from somewhere over towards Boston and he was mad on wigeon shooting.

Living in the county he could more or less pick his weather. He turned up on Kenzie one bitter evening in January 1930, driving his heavy old car, and dressed in a leather jerkin and riding breeches. He demanded that an immediate expedition be made for wigeon. Kenzie was, as a matter of fact, about to go out with cousin Kenny on the Lighthouse Marsh, Kenny being the hard case who didn't mind standing up to his knees in freezing water while wearing his ordinary leather boots, "so long as the old goonn keeps going off". Kenzie quickly agreed to making it a threesome.

It was an iron-hard frost. They drove out in the darkness along an old dirt road that was impassable by car in normal conditions, but the freeze-up had given it a temporary surface like tarmacadam. They drove right up to the sea wall, for Kenzie, out of youthful deference to the age of Mr Wright, "didn't want to walk him too far".

It was blisteringly cold, but soon the party forgot this, for the wigeon started to come in nicely. About ten o'clock the moon blacked out, which was excellent for shooting, since the birds were now outlined against the clouds. However, Kenzie was not entirely happy. "By Jove," he said to himself, "it's going to snow."

At midnight it started: at first, nice small crisp flakes, but then about one in the morning the flakes changed to soggy blobs the size of half a crown. The wind had shifted and Kenzie could smell a thaw coming. The wigeon were still obliging, but there were other matters on his mind. He rounded up Kenny and Mr Wright and ordered an immediate retreat to the sea wall. Before they reached the car, big snowflakes had given way to big raindrops. They were soon wet through. They had a tot of rum each and then tried to drive away. The car moved about a hundred yards along a dirt surface that was rapidly turning to slush and then went through the thawing ice crust into the morass underneath. Kenzie and Kenny got out and pushed and shoved, mud-covered and soaked, while Mr Wright dissolved his clutch in a solution of blue smoke. The car refused to budge.

"For God's sake pack up and come in," Mr Wright shouted at last.

They sat out the rest of the night in the back of the car, cold and wet to the skin. Kenzie had never been so frozen.

When morning came he walked back two miles in the continuing downpour to a farm. He found the ploughman and his opening remark is worth recording. "We're in a bit of trouble down the road, old feller..." he began. The ploughman produced a team of horses and pulled the derelict out in time for a late breakfast.

"And Mr Wright said to me: 'It's the only time I've ever seen you look cold, Kenzie.' And so it was. But he never took no harm. Mr Wright was a hard old case, and a very good wildfowler into the bargain."

Snowing again. More trouble with a car, and another hard case. This time, Kenneth Bromley. The freeze-up of 1947 had stacked the marsh creeks high with ice-floes, and the edge of the sea itself was dotted with pack-ice.

"The ice in the gutters was that thick that if you'd dropped through you'd have disappeared. Horry Savage, Bromley and I went far out on the frozen sands towards Fosdyke Cut. I dug three pits in the mud and we lay down in them to wait for the duck. By and by I spotted rafts and rafts of wigeon through the glasses, out on the edge of the tide. Beyond them I could see a ridge of something, though I couldn't make out exactly what it was. Well, the wigeon kept on drifting in and drifting in and I could see they were coming in up the channel close to where Mr Bromley and I was laying. They was thicker than hairs on a cat's belly. I said to Bromley: 'We'll just get one chance at these before the tide pushes us off. Let them get as close as they can and then when I say the word, get up and give them one.' It was ver' ver' exciting watching that great mass of duck float in. First one party would get up and fly over the main raft, and then another and so on, none of them going very far. At last I could see what was driving them. It wasn't only the tide. Right behind the birds was a great glacier of ice. Now they were within range. 'All right,' I yelled to Bromley, 'gi'e them one!' With that we both jumped to our feet and as the birds rose we went *plonk-plonk, plonk-plonk*—four barrels right through them. I could see we had plenty of birds down, and as the water was pretty shallow I plunged into the creek to pick them up. I hadn't gone twenty yards when I heard Bromley calling: 'For God's sake come out, Kenzie! Look behind you.' So I did, and then I saw right on top of me this great load of ice grinding down. I'd have disappeared under it in another few seconds. I only picked four of the birds. I counted thirty-two dead wigeon left out on the water. The saddlebacked gulls came from nowhere like dive-bombers. They were that hungry with the cold that they were carrying off whole wigeon to take them away and pluck them to pieces on the sands. But that wasn't the end of it. Mr Bromley at that time had a big old Lagonda sports car. By the time we reached it, it was snowing ver' ver' heavy. We hadn't gone a mile in the car when this big old Lagonda bogged down in a snow-drift. She wouldn't move no more than what Mr Wright's would all those years before. So we left the car and walked home twelve miles with the four wigeon. Next day Mr Bromley went out with a tractor and eight men to rescue the car, but at first they couldn't find it. It was buried that deep in a drift they had to prod for it with sticks."

Bromley was not put out by this experience, nor did Kenzie expect him to be. Kenzie's respect for this favourite client had been clinched by an incident on Terrington Marsh the previous winter.

When they set out that time the weather was similar to that which so basely betrayed Kenzie on the dirt road with Mr Wright: big flakes of snow turning to rain. This time the car had been left on a good hard surface several miles back. Everything was favourable for a big shoot. The moon was full and covered with fleecy cloud, and the making tide would push the wigeon up into the marsh pools. Kenzie was dressed for, as he thought, anything. "I had on two pairs of trousers, an oilskin, thigh boots, a "Ballyhava" hat and a waterproof underneathy hat. Well, we had a lot of shooting and we took a lot of cartridges with us, but by midnight I was wet right through. It was running out of the seat of my backside. I'd had enough, so I gradually drawed across to where Mr Bromley was. 'Hullo, Kenzie,' he said, 'what's up with you?'

" 'I thought of packing up, sir,' I said. " 'What on earth for?' he said.

"' 'Cos I'm a bit wet,' I said. 'Aren't you coming, sir?' I said.

" 'Not before I've shot out,' he said. " 'Well, I've had it, sir,' I said.

"And this is what he said then in these very words: 'Well,' he said, 'thank you. The great Lord Mackenzie Thorpe, the so-called professional wildfowler of Sutton Bridge, going off the marsh just because he's got a bit of wet in the arse of his trousers.'

" 'Ain't you coming, sir?'

" 'No, I'm not,' he said, and off he goes again. 'The great Lord Mackenzie Thorpe, etc...'

"So I left him to it, and an hour later Kenneth Bromley comes off the marsh with a great load of wigeon. He was a real hard case. When I tell you that in one week our bag was a hundred and fifty-five wigeon, sixty-two pinkfeet, two whitefronts, and forty-three shelduck, you'll see that he was a very good wildfowler indeed."

One of Kenzie's favourite parties came from King's Lynn. They were rather more than clients; they were kindred spirits. David Southgate, "a wonderful man with a gun, although he weighed twenty-two stone", was the substantial centre-piece of this group. His colleagues were the Frear brothers, John and Reg. To give you an idea of their capabilities: together with Kenzie they achieved what is probably the all-time record shoot along the Wash for one flight at curlew.

Now any wildfowler knows that curlew are impossibly wary birds. In fact, Kenzie Thorpe himself names the curlew as the most difficult bird to shoot. This makes interesting reading when put alongside the opinion of those countless game-shots who have named the high, gliding cock pheasant as the least destructible of birds.

Kenzie says: "The old curlew takes the cake without a doubt.

You can have been standing in a creek ankle-deep in water all the morning and suddenly a curlew comes at you. Flying into the wind or against it, he's equally hard to stop. For one thing, he's got better eyes than any bird, including a wood-pigeon. You can be ever so well hidden, but, the moment you make the leastest move to put your gun up, he throws himself upwards and sideways. Downwind he's certainly travelling at sixty miles per hour for a start, and it's nothing for his jink to throw him thirty yards or more across the sky in a few seconds. Even headwind he's not much easier. Maybe he's flying at forty-five miles per hour, but with the wind under his wings he'll jink even worse. Curlew are a bird that can look after theirselves. The best chance you've got is in the dawn or at dusk, or even by moonlight. Of course, you can call him if you know how, but you've got to be ver' ver' spry to make a big bag of curlew."

The two Frears, Kenzie and Southgate made a big bag. One morning when there was a twenty-seven-foot tide and all the marsh was covered, they intercepted the curlew coming off to feed on the white slugs in the big grass fields behind the sea wall. They picked up sixty-seven curlew, three mallard, one pintail, and one hare.

Shortly after the big curlew shoot, these same four were competing in a clay pigeon contest. Between rounds they went into a pub and there they met an old man called Jim Linden, whose claim to fame was that he had built his own houseboat.

"I reckon we could do that," said Kenzie. "We could park it down in the creek by Shep White's and use it as a wildfowling base. I know where we could get the stuff."

Kenzie at that time was working part-time at the timber merchant's in Sutton Bridge.

Reg Frear was a carpenter. Kenzie drew up his plans. The houseboat was to be based on his childhood memories of a Noah's Ark. Everything started out nice and legally. He saw the clerk at the timber yard and asked if he could have some cedar wood. The clerk agreed and told him to go and lay out what he needed. The bill was duly made out and paid, and it was arranged that this first load of planks should be collected early on Sunday morning.

The first consignment was taken to Kenzie's brother-in-law's place twelve miles from the sea. Later the boat would be moved down to the marsh by some means or other not yet fully made clear to the shipwrights themselves.

Work started at once. The following Sunday morning, and a number of Sunday mornings thereafter, a truck drew up at the timber yard at crack of dawn and started loading an unspecified number of two-by-fours, two-by-threes and inch-by-sixes.

"In the end," Kenzie recalls, "I didn't pay for all of it. In fact, I smuggled a bit out. And that's what I call knowing your whereabouts. Well, we finished her. She was sixteen foot long, seven foot wide and seven foot three high, and you could sleep four in her, and now we had to get her down to the marsh."

When the houseboat was finished Ivan Carlisle turned up from Wisbech with a lorry and two men. Kenzie had borrowed two trestles from the timber yard, also four three-by-nine planks, eighteen feet long. He had also talked the local basket factory into lending him some loading rollers.

With trestles and planks they built a sloping ramp up to the lorry, and then inched the houseboat, with the aid of the rollers, onto the commencement of the slope. But there manpower failed them. At this stage a next-door neighbour offered the loan of a tractor, and, by roping the houseboat round and pulling from the front of the lorry with the lines over the top of the cab, the overloaded ark was at last coaxed into mounting the lorry. However, it took the planks with it, trapping them between itself, the rollers and the lorry. Enough was enough for the time being: the boat was at least mobile.

Exhausted, the party piled into the lorry and drove away to the Shep White's end of the marsh, twelve miles distant. Kenzie had timed the operation to coincide with the highest spring tide available, but the schedule had gone to pieces so that when they reached the marsh the tide was far out.

They started to get the boat off, and it took four men two hours to free the trapped planks needed for an unloading ramp. Then they drove the lorry so that its nose was facing up the sea wall and rolled the boat off. When she was nearly down, Carlisle drove the lorry away and dropped the boat the last foot or so with a bump. The planks were still under her but this no longer mattered. From now on the tide would do the hard work.

Kenzie drove two stakes in and tied her up for the night. High tide was at seven next morning. When they came back next day the ark was launched and afloat in several inches of water. Carlisle and Kenzie pulled the planks out and poled her across the saltings with a fair wind and a dropping tide. They then tied her up against an embankment, where she remained for the next year. She'd be there still, but for the fact that farmer Ward, who grazed his cattle along this embankment, had never really recovered from his previous encounters with Kenzie in the latter's poaching days. Eventually Kenzie received a solicitor's letter, threatening action for trespass if he didn't move, so he set sail well down the marsh to the mean high-tide mark where the houseboat lies snug and secure today.

When the moon, wind, and tides are right, Kenzie takes his parties down to this tar-painted Noah's Ark and works the morning and evening flights from the houseboat, sometimes for a week on end. Everything aboard is shipshape and organized. Kenzie cooks the meals, and there are four bunks in which tired men can sleep with moderate comfort. She's as clean as a canal barge inside and stays that way because Kenzie, as captain of this strange craft, insists on rigid discipline. Waders are taken off outside and stuck upside down to dry on poles driven into the saltings for the purpose. On frozen marsh nights the Tilly lamp blazes away inside and the heat generated by this and four men becomes almost literally hellish.

One night when the snow was lying thick on the marsh outside and the atmosphere inside the houseboat was proportionately thick, the Tilly lamp suddenly extinguished itself with a most finite plop. There was no more oxygen left for it to burn. "If that had happened after we'd turned in," said Kenzie, who had noticed no distress until that moment, "they could have laid us out with the ducks and geese next morning."

The houseboat plays a large part in the story of one of Kenzie's most extraordinary wildfowlers and certainly one of the hardest cases of all.

In the winter of 1948 he received a letter from a farmer who wanted to shoot a wild goose. The farmer explained he'd shot plenty of pigeon and rooks, that he drove his own Land-Rover and tractor and was pretty active. The only trouble was that he had lost both legs and had artificial limbs. The difficulties of the project appealed to Kenzie, who wrote back saying that as far as he was concerned the trip was on.

The farmer arrived at two one afternoon, driving his Land-Rover. He was a big man and directly he got out of the vehicle and stumped in on artificial limbs, supporting himself with rubber-tipped sticks, Kenzie began to wonder whether he hadn't taken on too much. Kenzie loaded the gear aboard the Land-Rover and together they drove down to Shep White's *en route* for the houseboat. When they arrived at the sea wall, Kenzie announced his plan. "I'll carry you down to the boat about a quarter of a mile, sir, because you'll find it pretty soft going on those legs of yours."

"All right," said the legless wildfowler, "I'll take 'em off. I do better without them." He threw his legs in the back of the truck.

"Now," said Kenzie, "when the tide makes up this here creek, I'll come back in the gunning punt I keep against the houseboat and pick up the guns and all the gear."

Kenzie's houseboat tethered behind the seabank near Shep White's access.
Photo by courtesy of Bob Ashby.

It was heavy going across the green of the marsh with the legless man on his back, but well within Kenzie's physical range. When they reached the houseboat, the visitor swarmed aboard, minus his legs, with surprising ease. By the time Kenzie had punted up to the wall and brought back the gear, the legless man had made a pot of tea.

That evening flight, with a full tide, they went out to the stalk edges in the gunning punt and had a few wild shots at curlew and wigeon, but without success. This part of the operation had been easy, for it entailed no more than getting the visitor into the punt and poling down a creek. After supper Kenzie said politely:

"Which bunk would you like, sir?"

"The top bunk will do me."

"Fine, sir. Are you sure you can get up there?"

"It's quite simple," and the legless man swung himself up with his arms, rolling his body over.

"We'll need to be up early in the morning for the geese, sir. About half past three."

"That'll suit me." At three next morning Kenzie made the tea and woke his guest. He had laid his plans well. The geese would be crossing the sea wall a mile or two to the west of his present position, and this meant punting quite a long way up the marsh towards Fosdyke. The houseboat lay on one side of a deep, muddy creek. Over the creek was a high bank with an old roadway running along the top, and beyond that open water leading to the part of the marsh Kenzie planned to shoot. He had therefore left the boat the previous evening on the far side of this bank.

When they were ready to leave, Kenzie carried the guns and gear over the creek, now empty of water, and then came back for the legless wildfowler. Crossing the creek with the guns had been fairly hard going, but with a man on his back he sank at every step until he was knee deep in the ooze. "It tested me more than anything else in all my life." At last they made the far side, where he thankfully set the legless man down on the bank.

"Believe me, he went up that bank like a cat and got into the punt on the far side better than most ordinary men. The boat didn't go cockelly at all and I thought how nice that was. I've had normal men nearly upset a boat getting into it, standing on the coaming and not knowing how to go on at all. But this man, he didn't make the punt whip at all. It was beautiful. Well, we poled along about three mile in the dark with the curlew and waders bubbling and calling and the wigeon drakes whistling in the dark, and the legless wildfowler said to me how lovely and graceful it was that time of the morning, and I agreed. Soon I could hear the geese talking on the saltings, and I knew we couldn't go much further.

"I pulled the boat in by a bend and whispered to him to get out. He went up that bank, too, a slope of about eighty degrees and twenty-five feet high, quicker than a monkey, and down the far side. Then I got him on my back again and carried him to where I wanted him to shoot. He had a twelve-bore and I was using a big old eight-bore.

"The first lot of geese came off early. We heard them go by, but never saw them. I said: 'They was pretty close, sir, but not close enough.'

" 'It was lovely just to hear them,' he said.

" 'Hold on, sir. There'll be some more coming.'

"In the half-light I could see a little skein far off. And I ran doubled up to get close to the legless man and squatted down beside him. Then I started to call the geese. Well, they answered, and came in, and I thought they were going to present theirselves lovely, but at the last minute something made them swing a bit.

"I shouted out: 'This is the only chance we're going to get. Give 'em one, sir!'

"We both fired two barrels, and sure enough one goose dropped out stone dead. The tide was flapping the bank, so I knew the bird would drift in in about half an hour. But when I went to fetch it I nearly stepped on another goose, stone dead, too. It was stiff and cold, but fresh shot and must have been killed the day before. So I put it in the bag. When I got back I told the legless man.

" 'I wonder who shot it,' he said.

" 'Never mind who shot it,' I said. 'We've got it now and that's all that matters.'

"We poled back to the houseboat for breakfast and a preen-up and a rest. For evening flight, I dug my legless gunner a shallow pit on the marsh about quarter of a mile from the houseboat, and, when it came dusk, I carried him there and then went off to look for some wigeon myself. I left him my eight-bore to give him a bit of extra range.

"From where I was I could see the geese, about four or five thousand of them streaming in, not too high, over his position, but I only heard the eight-bore thump twice. When I got back to the houseboat he was already in it, though how he made it back there I can't think. Of course, he'd left the gun in his pit. I asked him how he'd got on.

" 'How did I get on?' he said. 'Those geese frightened me so badly I could only fire two shots. There were so many I thought they were coming down to worry me. They seemed to be pressing me right down into the ground with the noise they were making. It was colossal."
The news of this expedition slowly got around, for, much later, Kenzie received the following letter:

Madingley Hall
Cambridge
January 18, 1955

Dear Mr Thorpe,

Dr R. W. (Bill) Butler, whom I believe you took wildfowling on several occasions, tells me that you once managed to get a goose for a legless wildfowler.

I am in a similar position, being confined to a wheelchair by infantile paralysis. I do a great deal of shooting, mostly pigeon and duck, but have never managed to get a crack at a goose, and I am extremely keen to get one.

I would be most grateful to you if you could arrange something for me. I would bring one or two friends with me who would help with the chair, and suggest that the afternoon of Friday, February 3, ready for morning flight on Saturday (moon last quarter) or Friday, February 10 (new moon) would be suitable for the geese in the Holbeach St Matthew area, subject to your convenience and approval...

Yours sincerely,
W.H.W. INMAN

Kenzie wrote back saying that he was more than willing to have a go and received the following reply:

January 26, 1955

Dear Mr Thorpe,
　Thank you so much for your kind offer to help me shoot a goose.

　Although I am unable to walk at all, I am quite used to travelling over rough ground in the chair, and can crawl through wire fences etc. on my seat. My friend, Dr Gibbs, frequently carries me on his back (I only weigh nine stone) to a suitable position for flighting, and once in position I do not have to sit in the chair. I never have any camouflage problems, provided there is a creek or low hedge to sit behind.

　The evening of Friday, February 17, would suit us admirably, and I suggest that you expect us sometime in the afternoon or early evening on that day, so that we have plenty of time to lay our plans for the dawn flight on Saturday. I have no problem getting to Sutton Bridge as I drive my own car...

　　Yours sincerely,
　　W.H.W. INMAN

　It was snowing heavily on the day picked for the expedition. Mr Inman arrived with the doctor, a six-foot-four giant of a man. The time was four-thirty in the morning. The doctor took a collapsible wheelchair from the back of the Land-Rover and wheeled the paralysed man, who had lost the use of both legs, into Kenzie's kitchen.

　The plan, Kenzie explained, was to go to Terrington Marsh. If the snow wasn't too bad, he knew an approach along an old sea wall that would leave them the minimum distance to walk. The doctor assured him that a bit of snow didn't worry either them or their Land-Rover. But no sooner had they left the hard track and started along behind the sea wall than Kenzie began to wonder if their confidence wasn't overdone, for the vehicle pitched so badly in hidden ditches and ruts that he thought it was bound to overturn. The first flaw in the plan arrived in the form of a padlocked gate. Kenzie tried to lift it off its hinges but it was frozen solid. There was nothing for it but to leave the Land-Rover and lift the paralysed gunner, Mr Inman, over the top.

The other side, the doctor got Inman on his back, while Kenzie carried the guns and cartridges and some camouflage netting. Together they stumbled off down the snow-covered sea wall. The next obstacle in this nightmare cross-country event was a long shallow pan of soft mud that separated the wall from the marsh proper and was known locally, and graphically, as the "slaw pits". Kenzie led the way across the mud with the gear, the doctor and his human load following. After a few yards the doctor became completely bogged down, so Kenzie put down the gear and went back to pull him out. Safely on the far side, they were both so exhausted that they had to lay the paralysed man down in the snow. They made the final quarter of a mile out to the stalk edges with several stops for breath. There Kenzie dug a shallow pit in the side of a creek, put the paralysed gunner in it with a folded bag for a seat, stuck four posts around him and contrived a hide from camouflage net garnished with marsh grass. Kenzie and Dr Butler went further out onto the sands and dug themselves pits also.

When daylight came they all started to shoot. Kenzie and Dr Butler picked fourteen ducks apiece and were so hotly engaged that they barely noticed how far the tide had risen.

When they reached the paralysed man they found him sitting knee-deep in water. "Of course he couldn't feel nothing in his legs but his lips was blue with cold. He hadn't done too bad. We found four dead ducks and a curlew. We rubbed his hands a bit and though he could hardly speak with cold he seemed pretty happy. The Doctor carried him half-way back to the bank and I took him the rest of the way." In the Land-Rover they drank whisky in soup, rum in soup, and rum in tea, and were eventually warm again.

Two days later Kenzie received this letter:

February 20, 1955

Dear Kenzie,

We found your spade in the Land-Rover and are dispatching it to you by train; hope you will receive it soon.

I wonder if you had any luck finding the two torches. Should you be fortunate enough to find the flask as well,

I hope you will drink the contents before returning it to Dr Gibbs, for whom I believe it has a certain amount of sentimental value...

I shall definitely get in touch with you next season.

Yours sincerely,
W.H.W. INMAN

Kenzie had found the two torches and the flask which had been dropped at one of the many halts they had made for breath.

"I drank the contents, just like the paralysed wildfowler asked. And sent it back. I reckon that man had really got guts."

9

KENZIE THORPE IS a man who keeps records. Most of them are filed away in his head, in a photographic reference system that is surprisingly full and consistent. Others are on scraps of notebook paper, strangely spelled, curiously evocative of the time and the occasion. Mostly, the latter are comprised of statistics. Thus: "10 phesents, 3 heres, 1 widgin poached Caudwell's Nov. 14, 1941." They make an odd collection, these notes weirdly scrawled in more or less phonetic spelling. As far as figures are concerned I would warrant that they are accurate. One such jotting records that between 1953 and 1961 he went down to the marshes at morning and evening flight, and in the off-season simply to watch birds, no fewer than 3,453 times.

This makes an average of 430 visits a year. If one merely takes into account his years of professional wildfowling, beginning in 1928, this puts his total wildfowling experience at 14,620 expeditions, and there are the many excursions of his teens and early twenties to be added.

If Kenzie Thorpe is an original as far as poaching knowledge is concerned, then the same is certainly true of him as a wildfowler. He stems in direct line from the punt-gunners and flight-netters of the old fen days and much of their knowledge is his, together with an immeasurable amount he has added from his own observation and experience.

As with his fund of poaching lore, much of this first-hand observation, unless preserved in words now, will pass into blackness and oblivion when his turn comes to be laid out with the bag. Though some men may know more about ducks and geese in general, no one knows more about the comings and goings of wildfowl on the black fields and green saltings of Lincolnshire.

Again Kenzie must tell what he knows in his own way. Only the incidents which seem to illustrate the points he is making will be retold, if only for brevity's sake. For a good fen tale, told entirely by a fen-man, takes a deal of telling.

Kenzie speaking :

"When you arrive on the marsh in the dark, sit on the bank for a few minutes and see if you can hear the geese out on the sands. When you start down the green of the saltings, use a torch as seldom as possible. Stop every now and again and listen for the geese. In the dark you usually hear just a single call from an old bird, probably the gander. Get as close as you can to the pack in the dark. Geese on the Wash always flight towards the west, so when you're going out from the sea wall keep the geese on your right hand. At the first hint of dawn, the geese will start to call to one another pretty loud. Sometimes little parties will break away. This is ideal, particularly if there's a wind from the west. On a really rough morning they may keep coming off like this for half an hour or so.

"Never pick up your birds—provided you're sure they're dead—until the flight is over.

"Now for shooting geese at night when moon and tide are full. The geese will rest on the water until the tide leaves them high and dry. Then the moon will make them behave as though it's daylight, and they'll come inland to feed under the moon.

"Another way of coming to grips in the full moon is to follow the dropping tide out to the stalk edges. Follow the same rules as the day. Keep the geese on your right.

"Remember that on a moonlight night the geese won't flight from the marshes unless they're left high and dry. Geese will sometimes come inland to feed on the first quarter of the moon. Once in my time I've seen them flight on the Northern Lights. I've even known them fly inland on bright starlight.

"If the moon sets about three, the geese will often return onto the marshes from their inland feeding grounds, and then they're dead easy to call. You've got enough light to shoot for about three-quarters of an hour after the moon sets.

"You can sometimes get some wonderful shooting off the sea wall on a rough or misty night. If the first skein pass wide of you, run like hell to get under the flight-line as the next party will probably pass close."

It was a November half-moon. The party consisted of two Yorkshire wildfowlers and Kenzie. They had waited at a duck flash where Kenzie had spotted feathers and droppings the previous day. He was expecting the birds to come in to it under the moon. After three hours nothing had happened except that the wind, which was bitter, had dropped away and a slight ground haze was forming. The change of wind brought the sound of geese. A big pack lay somewhere out on the sands. About one o'clock in the morning some of the geese became airborne and flew across the sea wall inland to feed on the moonlit fields. Kenzie gathered his gunners and led them at a sprint half a mile along the top of the wall to where he judged the geese had crossed. Sure enough, other parties began to flight, and, perhaps confused by the ground haze, kept low. By two a.m. when the inland flight had stopped they had shot nine geese from the sea wall.

Kenzie again :

"When the geese are feeding in and under the moon they will sometimes stop there for a month at a time, using one big field to roost on and another to feed on. Instead of going out to the sands at dusk they'll simply fly to their roosting field. This is the time to go after them with decoys.

"Decoys *can* be used on the marshes but the visibility must be really bad. Inland, on young wheat or on potato fields, they can be deadly. You put your field of 'coys out within range of the dyke where you're hiding. The wind must be at your back, so that you are between the wind and the decoys. The geese have got to turn into the wind to land. Never put your decoys out too regular. Dot them about and don't place them all facing directly into the wind. You never see real geese or ducks lined up like soldiers on parade. As soon as the first skein appears, start to call. If they show any sign of going down on a part of the field where your decoys aren't, then you've got to call very heavy to pull them in to you. Mostly you use this method in the early morning when the geese are coming off the sands. Of course you must know which fields the geese are using and that's where all the study comes in.

"For decoying you can use dead birds, if you have saved some from the day previous: lay them head to wind and fan their tails out a bit. The white in the tail seems to attract other birds. I told you how I once shot birds with Horry when using white paper with a clod of earth on each piece. I do believe the birds took that white paper for the spread tail coverts of feeding geese.

"When you're decoying you must keep dead still, for though the geese are concentrating on the decoys they can soon spot anything suspicious. But I can tell you that you've got to put in hours and hours of studying if you want to get big bags of geese. When the geese are flighting between inland roosting and feeding fields you can keep shooting for hours sometimes, particularly over decoys. I've made some big slaughters this way but those days are ending for me. Nowadays I think twenty-five geese is plenty for four guns to shoot."

On a Sunday morning in November 1952 Kenzie had taken a Dr Beatty from King's Lynn inland to decoy geese. The doctor had done plenty of shooting but had never bagged a pinkfoot. At about six in the morning a nice little flight developed, the first skein swinging in to Kenzie's call. Both guns dropped a right and left. Despite the fact that there weren't great numbers of geese about, the total pick-up was eleven birds. Kenzie was certain that the area held more geese than he had seen, so, when the flight was over, he asked the doctor whether he would drive him round the district on a reconnaissance. Before long they heard numbers of geese and found a flock of about five hundred feeding on a stubble field belonging to a farmer whom Kenzie knew quite well. Kenzie went up to the farm and met the farmer's son. "Do you mind if I have a go at these here old geese?" he asked.

"Not if I can have a go with you," said the young man.

"All right then. Tomorrow morning. We'll want four guns."

"I can bring a friend," said the farmer's son.

"Good," said Kenzie, "and I'll get Mr Carlisle from Wisbech, for Doctor Beatty here has to be at work tomorrow."

They started out early next morning. Kenzie had brought Canada goose decoys given him by some American fowlers, and, though these were over-size, he had repainted them in pinkfoot colours. He'd also had some heavy gauge steel wire cut into short lengths, for he had a feeling that he might have a use for it.

The flight started at six in the morning. Kenzie called the first three geese in, and all were shot. Then a skein of four, and four came down. Next six geese, not one of whom got through the barrage. Kenzie set the dead birds up with their heads propped on the steel wires, and for the next six hours he was shooting, running out to put up decoys, and calling fresh geese in.

"We shot them very sporting, only taking the hard, fast birds, but when we'd shot out at midday the farmer's son had to fetch a tractor and a trailer to carry the bag back. While we were sharing out the geese, fresh birds were still coming in to land.

"I caught a terrible chill running out, getting hot, and then sitting down in the freezing cold, and I was laid up in bed for a fortnight."

They had shot seventy-eight geese—far, far too many.

"I use three kinds of 'coys. The first are my most successful allrounders though they're bulky, but light, to carry. Whatever 'coys you're using, you only need six. Geese don't notice the faults so much with six, but above that number they begin to spot the mistakes. I make my solid 'coys out of wire netting. You need a strip two foot six long and about the same wide. Fold it to the shape of a goose. This takes a bit of doing, but you soon get the idea of shaping the head and neck. You stuff the inside with very tightly rolled up sheets of newspaper. You want about thirty or forty *News of the World*s to make one pinkfoot. You buy some cheap white calico and stick or stitch it all over the outside of the wire. Then you paint the outside of the calico with flat paint. Buy flat paint to start with and mix in paraffin which takes the shine out of any paint. The calico does the rest. Paint them very goose-like. I even put the black nail on the beak and the pink band across. Geese are sometimes ver' ver' suspicious, though not always. You can leave the calico white for the underneath parts, but in time this will get very dirty so you'd better paint it white. Get your colours right and use a bird book—dark forehead, sooty brown head, grey back, white in front, and so on.

"Flat pear-shaped decoys are much simpler. They come in handy for moonlight flighting inland. They can be cut from marine plywood which stands up to any weather. They want to be one foot three inches long and ten inches wide. Paint them grey all over and give the tail a white tip. Leave the tail part pointed, for, when you come to set them out, you want to stick this in the ground so that the 'coy is tilted up a few degrees to the earth.

"Set out your decoys on the field so that your birds are coming to your decoys from the direction of the moon, if you possibly can. Geese on the Wash flight from the east, that is from the rising moon, to the west. Get your back to the wind and look towards the lightest part of the sky. Call when you hear the geese coming and leave off calling once they spot the 'coys.

"Silhouette decoys are nice and light but they have the disadvantage that the geese can't see them when they're head on to them. As geese land into the wind this means that you've got to set them out crosswind. It's all right when there's a gale blowing and the birds want to get their feet down quickly. Then they see the 'coys sideways on and drop in first time. But when it's still the geese generally have a bit of a fly round first. They see the silhouette 'coys as they come in, and then, as they turn first time round, the 'coys suddenly disappear from view. That's when you're liable to lose your geese altogether. Perhaps they think the decoys have been disturbed and have flown and that this is no place for them. But when you know how, using decoys, particularly the pear-shaped or the solid ones, is ver' ver' simple. You can even get geese to feed among the decoys."

One night Kenzie had three American gunners out with him. They were decoying inland from a dyke and had shot fourteen geese by the early hours of the morning. Then the moon clouded over, the geese stopped coming and the party decided to pack up. One of the Americans had not shot a goose that night. They were just leaving their hiding-place when a single bird dropped out of the clouds and came in to land among the decoys which were still on the field. Kenzie whispered to the gooseless American: "Come on then, sir, there's your chance."

Kenzie shouted: "Get up then and give the gentleman a shot!"

The goose went on feeding.

Kenzie took off his rucksack and threw it out among the decoys.

Kenzie making a brew at his houseboat.
Photo by courtesy of Mr & Mrs J. T. Amos

The goose merely responded by flying four or five yards away. At last Kenzie got out of the dyke and the bird took wing. The American shot his goose. "Sometimes in bad light," Kenzie explained, "goose among decoys can act ver' ver' simple."

Again...
On a moonlit field during a snow flurry three geese came in together to the flat pear-shaped decoys. Ivan Carlisle, the regular from Wisbech, and Kenzie got two of them and the third towered away. There were no other geese about so Kenzie went out to pick up the two dead birds and set them up as additional decoys. As he was walking back through the field of decoys the third goose called. Kenzie called back, and the goose answered. Kenzie judged that the survivor was coming back fast. He hadn't time to make it back to the cover of the dyke so he threw himself down amid the decoys, still holding the two dead birds. The goose swooped in to land, put its feet down, and dropped within five yards of him. Kenzie watched it spellbound. It had its neck stretched up which meant that it was uneasy. Kenzie shouted to his son. The goose took off and was shot as it climbed out of the field.

Kenzie on weather: "You've got to watch conditions all the time. You get to feel when there's a change coming. Sometimes it will be for the better, sometimes for the worse. You've got to know what it will do to the fowl, and if it's a change for the better (which usually means bad weather) you've got to take advantage of it quickly."
In January 1944 Kenzie was out by himself after wigeon in a bitter cold spell. Morning flight had been very disappointing for the wind had dropped away almost to nothing. The total bag by midday was three wigeon and one mallard, and, since he was living off the gun at that time, this was a pretty slim look out. He went back to the sea bank for a bite to eat and was just drinking a cup of tea when he felt the wind strike differently on his cheek. It had started to blow from the east. This, Kenzie knew, would disturb the duck on the sea and send them in for shelter. As he hurried down the marsh he could see little parties of wigeon making up from the Norfolk side of the Wash towards Northern Creek. Kenzie got down into the creek for cover, and now it was freezing so hard that the splashes of water turned to

ice as they hit his Wellingtons. The sun was just going as a long stalk brought him close to an enormous pack of wigeon. They were, he remembers, "closer than spines on a hedgehog's back". This could be a very big shoot. But then in the last light he saw a party of eight mallard flicker in to pitch on the creek edge between him and his quarry. Now the trouble with mallard is that they are both noisy and cautious. If he scared them, their take-off and alarmed quacking would certainly put the wigeon up in a cloud. So he stood dead still in the creek bottom for five minutes just moving his hand over the top very slightly so that the mallard would see it, become uneasy but without panicking, and gradually shift away. Just when the light was nearly gone this ruse worked. "The mallard flushed off without a murmur." Immediately he rose out of his creek. So did the pack of wigeon. Kenzie fired two barrels and picked up seventeen wigeon and two mallard. "Not bad for government trap-shooting cartridges loaded with number sixes."

"Ducks will decoy just as easily as geese, and one decoy, the mallard, does for them all-teal, pintail, shoveller, wigeon. But you don't often shoot ducks on the fields, as you can geese, and you've got to 'coy them out on the marshes where there isn't much cover. Shooting a lot of duck on the marshes depends on being well hidden. You've got to take your time about making concealment. The best thing of all is a pit. It's wet and muddy in a pit, but you can take something to lie on, and from a well-dug pit you can shoot a lot of birds."

At the end of January 1954 Kenzie had four good shots with him. It had been snowing for a week and the saltings were six feet deep in places. The wind was strong and from the sea and everything was rough enough for a big bag of duck. The birds certainly wouldn't face the buffeting the east wind would give them out to sea and sooner or later would seek the stalk edges. Kenzie took his party in the dark of this chilly morning up to a place beyond Shep White's called Duck Hole. Here was a shallow muddy pan surrounded with spartina grass which would be covered with a few inches of water at full tide. Kenzie dug his gunners and himself five well-prepared pits and set out twenty-five rubber mallard decoys on the flat pan. The ducks started to come at seven a.m., just as it was getting light, and kept it up until two in the afternoon when the party ran out of cartridges. The pick up was: fifteen mallard, forty-four wigeon, three geese, five teal, two pintail, twenty-eight shelduck, seven golden-eye, and one curlew, and nearly as many birds had dropped through the snow-crust and disappeared. The party had to carry the bag two and a half miles to the cars and grumbled and groused all the way. "That's the sort of thing you're up against if you're a professional wildfowler. If they don't see no fowl they wonder where the birds are, and if they shoot a lot they don't want to carry them. You've got to be prepared to work hard if you want sport, and they wouldn't have had no sport at all if I hadn't dug those five pits. And that was work I can tell you."

Next day the weather held and the party shot as many duck from the same pits.

"Duck decoys will sometimes attract other birds, even geese. I suppose it's just a sign to them that everything is safe down below on the ground."

In January 1943 Kenzie was still shooting a lot of shelduck. He got 45s. apiece for them, even though they are not the best of eating: in fact, they are some of the worst, at least as far as wildfowl is concerned. They received protection in 1954, though their rank taste and sinewy carcasses should have been enough long before that to warrant them safe passage. However, as Kenzie's record shows, some people will eat anything. It's only fair to point out, though, that he sold his shelduck during the rationing days of the War.

He had gone down to the Lighthouse Marsh, taking with him four dead shelduck from the previous day's shooting. As always when decoying with dead birds, he chose those whose plumage looked the least muddy and ruffled. He also took the precaution of painting the bills pink, for all ducks, and especially shelduck, lose colour in the beak after death. He started shooting about half past two in the afternoon and was beginning to pile up a score when he saw sixty brent geese sweeping in from the sea. The brents spotted the dead shelduck and swung in towards them, making, as Kenzie recalls, "their beautiful noise". Notwithstanding, Kenzie put two barrels straight through them and knocked out eight geese. Three of these were the light-bellied variety, very rarely seen on the Wash. The bag to those four original decoys was twenty-nine shelduck, eight brent, and one wigeon.

"I can call most wildfowl. Whoopers, all grey geese, barnacles and brent, mallard, wigeon, teal, curlew, whimbrel, godwit, knot, redshank, greenshank, grey, golden, and green plover, snipe, French and grey partridges, pheasants, and of course the old hare.

"To call birds you want bad visibility and plenty of cover, especially for curlew. You can call curlew up to the end of December. After that they won't come to the call at all. With redshank in the first part of the season you want to show yourself now and again, so that the birds will come and mob you. Wigeon calling is done chiefly at last light, dawn, and in the moonlight. You can only call them in good visibility if you've got decoys out. Mallard are best called on their feeding grounds at morning flight but the weather wants to be bad. Golden plover will come at any time, even in bright sunshine. Grey plover will come to a call when flying on the tide edge. You can even bring in bunches of knot with a call. Shelduck can't be called, even if you match their noise ever so perfectly. Pinkfeet can be called quite simply on their feeding grounds but you can only swing them off a flightline to and from the marsh when it's foggy or they are in little parties.

"Calling's something you've got to start early on in life. With pinkfooted geese the gander has a fairly high call, but the female is much lower. The important call is the gander's because he does most of the talking to keep the skein together."

A fowler called Bob Ashby used to go out with Kenzie but he had never had a shot at a goose. "Look here, Kenzie," he said, "if you can get me a goose next time I'm booked to go fowling with you I'll give you ten pounds."

"You will, sir?"

"I most certainly will."

When Ashby came back in November 1947 he said nothing about his offer but simply remarked that he was very keen to get his first goose. They went out far down the sands on their first morning flight and at first light it looked as though Ashby's luck was going to be out again. The usual flight of saddlebacked and herring gulls flew in from the sea at dawn, but no geese. However, among the gulls, far off on the tide-line, Kenzie picked out three geese. He called with the high imperious bark of the gander and the little skein faltered and changed course. He called and called and the birds came right in. Kenzie held his fire and waited for Ashby. He fired at last, and right and left sent both birds crashing to the sand. The third bird flew on and then wavered as if in doubt which way to fly. Then it called. Kenzie recognized an indecisive bird and called it frantically. To his surprise the goose turned and came back towards the guns. Ashby fired again and got his third goose. Kenzie had never seen anything quite like it in all his wildfowling days.

When they got back to Sutton Bridge, Kenzie examined the three geese and found his answer. The gander was an old bird and the two others were goslings. The survivor had felt lost without his flight leader and had called for help, only to have Kenzie answer him. He had turned back believing the gander was still alive and looking for him.

"What about my ten pound now, sir?" Kenzie asked. Ashby paid him a fiver, which both surprised and satisfied him.

"If you've got another fowler out with you, always in the half-light make sure you know exactly where he is. I've never yet had an accident in my parties on the marsh, though I once came close to it, and then the only reason I didn't was because I acted ver' ver' cautious. I knew something wasn't quite right."

Kenzie had gone out in the gunning punt for morning flight with one of his regulars, Harry Brown from Yorkshire. Brown knew what he was up to and, on his day, was a good shot. It was bitterly cold and this may have been what caused Brown to move out of position. Kenzie stationed him in Northern Creek, having watched seven geese fly into the marsh a little further down. The tide was dropping and the plan was to follow the creeks out to sea, walking on the hard shell bottom. Just as it got light, two duck came for Kenzie. He dropped them both with a right and left. Both had seemed to be dead in the air. He'd just made up his mind to leave them, rather than climb out of his creek to pick them up and risk disturbing other birds, when he caught a movement out of the corner of his eye.

"By Jove," Kenzie thought to himself, "one of them was winged after all." He could see this duck in the half-light bobbing about on the edge of a nearby creek not twenty yards away. Mercy as well as expediency dictated that this runner be given the quietus quickly. Kenzie took the three-inch cartridge loaded with fours out of his right barrel and put in a cheaper two-and-a-half-inch loaded with sixes. He

was just about to draw back and give the duck one when something made him stop and call out:
"Is that you, Mr Brown?"
"Yes, it is, why?"
"I thought your head was my duck. I was just about to shoot you, and I'd very probably have killed you, Mr Brown."
"By Jove, Kenzie, so you might have!"

"Clothing is important on the marshes. Don't wear gloves. They're dangerous with a gun. You're likely to let drive without meaning it. At best, you'll miss chances. If you get cold, put your hands in the cold salt water. Don't dry them. Just shake them. They'll tingle and you'll not be cold for the rest of the day. Never wear a peaked cap. You can't see the birds above your head without waving your head about all over the place, and a flash of pink flesh puts fowl off quicker than anything. I use a woolly 'Ballyhava,' white for preference, or muddy as it gets to be after a time. Don't tie your Wellingtons on round the ankles. If you do, keep a good sharp knife with you. If you get stuck in mud you may be glad to get out of your boots in a hurry. Your best coat to wear is a three-quarter coat, just above the knees. It wants to be olive-green colour for morning and evening flight. Under it you want sweaters, as many as you need. And as you get very hot walking out to flight, then it's a good thing to take your sweaters off and put them in your rucksack—don't use a side bag; they're hopeless on the marshes—so that you can put them on when you begin to cool off. There's nothing worse than getting hot and then lying about without proper covering. Even if you've got a long wait ahead, don't be tempted to have a nap. That's the worse thing for health you can possibly do."

The two Frears and David Southgate had gone to flight the geese with Kenzie at Dowsell Bank, a lonely place which lies on the boundaries of Lincolnshire, Norfolk and Northamptonshire. They had some trouble finding the fields Kenzie had heard the geese were using. In the end they had to walk five miles over muddy plough and stubble to reach the flighting grounds. Kenzie set out the decoys, but, when the moon came up, the geese, who could be heard talking on a field not half a mile away, refused to move. Kenzie left his three colleagues and set out to shift the geese to them. After a long stalk he put the geese up, but they insisted on coming back to their resting-ground in little skeins. Kenzie began to shoot. By the early hours he had fourteen pinkfeet to his own gun. When he came to take the birds off the field, the going was so soft that he had to make two trips. He was surprised that he had heard comparatively little shooting from the others. He slogged his way back to the field where he had left them. There he found the decoys sitting out in the moonlight, also seven dead birds, the three fowlers' bags, guns, and cartridges, but no sign of the fowlers themselves.

He had waited half an hour on the bank, drinking rum and cocoa, when he saw the three men approaching.

"Where the hell have you been?"

"We got tired and cold so we went to have a sleep in a straw-stack."

"Well, you're daft. You missed a fine chance at geese."

They gathered the birds and decoys and then Kenzie and Reg Frear set off five miles across country to bring the car as close as they could to the bank. David Southgate, the twenty-two-stone man, now returned to the straw-stack.

Two days later Southgate, a redoubtable and experienced wildfowler, was ill in bed.

"The moral," says Kenzie sadly, "is don't never go to sleep in a straw-stack—or anywhere else—when out wildfowling."

Southgate developed pneumonia and was laid up for ten weeks.

Kenzie on guns: "I've tried them all. A three-inch magnum twelve with twenty-eight-inch barrels, heavily choked, tops the lot. Use BBs for geese and number fours for duck. Four-bores, eights, and tens are more trouble than they're worth on the saltings."

In January 1947 Kenzie took his son along with Ivan Carlisle to try for geese at Ingatestone Fen. They were shooting over flat pear-shaped decoys on the first quarter of the moon. There weren't many geese about but those that were flighting came well spaced in small parties, an ideal arrangement. Carlisle and Kenzie were both shooting with three-inch magnum twelve-bores loaded with BB. Three geese came in over the decoys and Kenzie gave his classic fire order: "Right, sir, gi'e em' it." Carlisle and Kenzie fired four barrels without touching a feather. The geese climbed and went away high over Thorpe junior, who knocked one stone dead out of the sky with a twenty-bore game-gun. The story proves nothing, except that no gun is any good to you unless you hold it straight.

"Fog can be very useful for goose shooting as they don't much care to take off early, and when they flight it will be in small parties. Of course, an incoming tide will persuade them to get up, but they don't want to fly on foggy mornings. In fog they make a peculiar lost noise. It's a sort of humming, and it's rather weird. That's the time to call them, and they'll really come to you because they are lost."

When Kenzie shone his torch out of the door of the houseboat at four a.m. that November morning his beam was met by a wall of fog. He could just see that the tide was full in the creek ten yards away. He woke Harry Brown, that same Harry Brown he had come perilously close to shooting on a previous trip, with:

"It's a thick fog, sir. Come on. Get up. We're going to get a good shoot."

Brown's companion in the top bunk refused to stir. "What's wrong with him?" Kenzie was astonished. "He's often like this in the morning," said Brown. "Well, he don't want to be like it this morning. It's a wonderful morning for geese." However, the second wildfowler stayed in bed while Kenzie and Brown pushed off down the creek on the ebb in the gunning punt. Before long Kenzie found himself losing his way, since the fog was thick and the marsh still covered. So he drove in the pole and tied up until the tide dropped a fraction. When the top of the spartina grass showed through, he said to Brown: "There's the creek. We're right over it." They poled down the rapidly emptying channel and then abandoned the boat and set out on foot towards the noise of the geese who were making their worried, humming fog sound.

Conditions were ideal. The geese kept taking off in small skeins and cruising around trying to find their bearings. When they called, Kenzie answered, and very often they came in to offer a shot. By breakfast-time they had shot fourteen geese. They piled them in the punt and walked back to the houseboat.

"The other young gentleman was still asleep, and serve him right if he couldn't get up for a lovely morning like that. Later on I walked out and brought the punt and the geese back on the making tide within ten yards of the houseboat, and that's what I call a bit of gentleman fowling."

"When I take people out fowling I never 'pologize to them if they don't get no sport. Wildfowling is like that. It's the fact that you can't be sure even on the most likely days what's going to happen that makes it so exciting. Anyway, I work my best to put my guns in the way of a bit of shooting, and if they don't get it, well I reckon nobody can't do more for them. So I never 'pologize if they've got clean barrels, and I expect them to pay their pound a flight just the same."

In 1959 Kenzie was out with a choleric major who occasionally shot at Sandringham. The major was a regular customer but he always demanded to be taken out alone. This, of course, was to Kenzie's disadvantage, as he only got one fee. But then the major was "a very jealous gun".

Kenzie was certain that the geese would come to a certain potato field, and he took the major there on an icy dawn and set eight decoys out in the field. After three hours the major had shot a brace of mallard. He kept on saying "a very disappointing morning, Kenzie. Very disappointing." Kenzie thought to himself: "It's about time I shut him up." Aloud he said to the major: "Look here, sir, you know a bit about wildfowling. Now just you be patient a spell."

The major grunted, then said : "Where are we going this evening?"

"Same field, sir."

"Don't be silly, man. It's no damn' good."

"You be round at my house at three o'clock," Kenzie said firmly.

About four o'clock that afternoon Kenzie positioned the major in the same dyke. Within half an hour the geese came piling in, five hundred birds in all. They shot fifteen geese before the flight stopped. Kenzie gave the major seven to carry to the car and took eight himself. All the way back to the car the major groused about the weight of the bag.

Next morning they left home at four a.m. and went to a stubble field where the geese were resting during the day. The ground was frozen so hard that Kenzie had to use a hammer and chisel to make holes for the decoys. That morning the bag was fourteen geese, though this time the major insisted on driving the car on to the field to collect the fallen. That afternoon on the same potato field where they had shot the fifteen, they got another five. The third morning they were back on the stubble and bagged nineteen and a mallard. At one moment Kenzie had three dead in the air at the same time.

The major complained: "Give me a chance, man."

"They was on my side, sir. They was my birds. That's the way it is, and you know that."

The score for those five flights was fifty-three geese and three mallard.

"Normally, I'd have been glad to get such shooting for my guns, but these geese weren't appreciated. Anyway, it shows you how simply you can decoy geese once they've gone inland both to roost and feed—if you know their tricks, that is."

"You may think it's disgraceful to shoot geese or ducks when they're sitting on the ground. Well, I'll tell you. Sometimes, when it's too easy, I'd agree with you. But the thrill of a long hard stalk is ver' ver' colossal. If you work hard for a sitting shot through slush and snow, then it's worth it. But you don't get nothing from it if you don't have to work hard hardly at all."

In a desk in the little room where he paints and keeps his bird books, Kenzie has a special drawer for goose rings. There are now 145 of them; "a very nice collection indeed". Several were placed on the birds, in the first instance, in Iceland, by his old employer Peter Scott. Invariably Kenzie reports the numbers stamped on these rings to the Wildfowl Trust or to the ringing authority. To some ornithologists a dead goose may be a minor tragedy, but it is also a source of information. This is the story of Kenzie's first ring, a product of a sitting shot and a hard stalk.

Ivan Carlisle had been out moonlight flighting with him on the marsh. As they drove back, Kenzie suddenly asked Carlisle to stop the car because he thought he could hear geese. "They're on that potato field over there," he told his client. They pulled the car onto the grass verge and got out their guns. Kenzie led the way along an intricate system of dykes that were certainly slushy. They could hear the geese very plainly, but, just as it seemed they must be within shot, a bank cut short their progress along the dyke bottom. Kenzie cursed, then examined the bank. He found a field drain two feet wide running through the obstacle ahead of them. "It's like this, sir," he hissed at Carlisle. "We've got to crawl through this here tunnel." They crawled. When they emerged at the other end they were "all cobwebbed up". Kenzie started off again straight away, however, and at a cracking pace. He recalls: "The geese were now right next to us over the top of the bank. They were making that beautiful humming noise. I said, 'Right, sir, gi'e em' it,' and we nipped over the top of the bank and fired four barrels as they rose. I got three and Carlisle two. One was my first ringed bird. And that's what I call a worthwhile stalk you don't feel ashamed of. It was ver' ver' dark in that tunnel."

Kenzie on pigeon: "I shoot a lot of wood-pigeon now, mostly on the pea fields. I've had bags of a hundred and fifty in a day to my own gun. Pigeon are as wary as wildfowl, if not more so. Just as when you're decoying duck, a good hide is essential. Build it up well at the back, so that it hides your outline, and only look out in one direction—that is, over the decoys. I much prefer using dead birds for decoys, but they must be perfect: not a feather out of place and not a spot of blood on them. The way to keep them perfect is to get an old nylon stocking and cut the foot out. You can slip two dead pigeons down into this, and provided you draw them out head first, you'll never ruffle a feather.

"Put your decoys out so that some of them are crosswind as well as headwind. Then the breeze will get under the tails of the crosswind birds and cock them up every now and again so that it looks as though they're feeding. I use old bicycle spokes tucked under their chin, or stuck through the crops, to hold them up naturally in a feeding position, and they look just like the real thing, which is important.

"If I'm shooting with a .22 rifle as well as a twelve-bore I cut the eyelids of the dead birds,[1] for a pigeon landing among the decoys won't stay for a sitting shot if it sees the decoy with its eyes closed.

"If I'm using lofters I put them in a sitting tree, that is to say a dead tree, or a tree with dead boughs, in which the birds are used to sitting. I think they like these dead trees, both because they can see danger better from them and because they can make a quick getaway. They're ver' ver' cunning birds. If you have to use artificial decoys make sure you've got the biggest ones possible and see that the white collar is ver' ver' plain. Don't listen to tales about using big shot for pigeon. Number six is plenty, and that is what I use all the time. And you can shoot a lot of pigeon if you do what I tell you.

"The day will come when I shall pack up shooting the geese altogether and just shoot pigeon. I'm beginning to think that pinkfooted geese ought to have only a two-month open season, in November and December."

[1] Kenzie's views on pigeon shooting coincide almost exactly with those of that greatest of experts, Archie Coats, professional pigeon-shooter from Hampshire, but with one notable exception. This is Kenzie's insistence on "exact imitation" as far as decoys are concerned. It has long been held by countrymen that it is necessary to cut the eyelids off dead pigeons—a gruesome business at best—in order to fool live pigeons. Coats shoots well over 10,000 birds a year, and never worries about unruffled plumage, let alone eyelids, although he admits that stuffed pigeons with well-preserved feathers are the best thing to start a shoot off. However, it doesn't do to discount all rural "old wives" tales, as some of them have a nasty habit of confirming later scientific observation. With respect to Kenzie, though, I must say that I entirely share Coats's view. I've seen pigeons happily strutting amid big stands of decoys, some being propped up, others just being laid out anyhow. I have seen them feeding amid clouds of loose feathers from fallen birds. Admittedly, this has been later on in a decoy shoot, when there have been perhaps thirty or forty dead birds set out. By then it is the *number* of decoys that counts. At the outset it may be lifelike representation that matters to get the pigeons going, but I doubt whether eyelids ever count.

10

UNTIL THE MOMENT at which I wrote these words Kenzie had shot, or had helped others to shoot, 3,700 geese. By the time you read this the total may be considerably more. The present total world population of pinkfeet is about 45,000. In his best season, 1951, Kenzie shot 414 geese, or nearly 1½ per cent of the world supply. Now there is no doubt that this is far too many geese for one man to kill, and I think that Kenzie himself is beginning to realize it. People have said this to him, but possibly not always in the way that would have most effect. You have to remember that for Kenzie the geese are not only a way of making a living, they are also, that much overworked phrase, a way of life. Sometimes I think that you might as well try to tell a big black cat that it really should stop catching mice.

Peter Scott has tried to persuade Kenzie to hang up his goose gun, but he, of all people, is, I think, least likely to make the conversion. The influence of Scott on Kenzie has been an interesting one. To begin with there is a certain physical resemblance, and Kenzie is pleased when people notice it. One of the surprisingly few references to Kenzie Thorpe in Scott's autobiography describes how, when Scott was away from the East Lighthouse at Sutton Bridge, Kenzie borrowed his paints and easel "and was quite ready to be taken for myself". I'm perfectly certain that this is true for there were many things about Scott which Kenzie both envied and admired, not the least of which was Scott's ability to paint wildfowl. There were marked incompatibilities between employer and employee in those early days. Kenzie felt Scott, as a young man, was inclined to be pompous, and he may well have been right. Certainly, as has been shown, there were tiffs in which Kenzie as Scott's employee no doubt exceeded himself, but then he is a fen-man and fen-men have a rugged individuality which sometimes does exceed itself.

On Kenzie's side there were certainly faults. To him Scott was a gilded young man fresh from Cambridge who could afford to pay £50 a pair for red-breasted geese and yet only offered Kenzie one pound for a bean goose which he had caught on the marsh—a fact which still rankles. Though admitting that Scott was the best boss he ever had, Kenzie undoubtedly took the standpoint of a have-not looking at a have. As a paid employee Kenzie was perhaps not strictly entitled to these views or justified in holding them, but hold them he did. Another irritant was that in those days Scott was shooting great numbers of geese himself, both in the punt with the big gun and with a twelve-bore, and he didn't care for Kenzie shooting on his time. All these things have a bearing on Kenzie's later reaction to a letter from the Director of the Severn Wildfowl Trust asking him to think about giving up goose shooting.

When Scott left the Lighthouse for the War in 1939 he told Kenzie that he would be back and that he would have the finest collection of wildfowl in the world. Kenzie has said sadly: "And so he has, but I'm not working for him."

Kenzie undoubtedly expected to be summoned to the New Grounds, Slimbridge, to help as he had helped in the old days, but Scott had changed even if Kenzie hadn't. He had practically stopped shooting. Wildfowler had become leading conservationist. Prince Hal had become Henry V, and there was no place for a Lincolnshire Falstaff at the New Grounds. The decision—it is probable that it did not even become a consideration let alone a decision—the decision was Scott's privilege, and my own opinion is that he was right not to ask Kenzie to work for him again from every point of view, his own and Kenzie's. Not only would Kenzie have been like, if you will excuse the phrase, a duck out of water, but he would not have fitted into a Wildfowl Trust set-up. This was no longer a question of keeping a hundred or so birds in pens by rule of thumb. This was now scientific study of wildfowl habits and movements, and the University rather than the marsh was the training ground.

One night in 1947 Kenzie met Scott driving along the main road at Sutton Bridge. Perhaps Scott was on a trip to revive old memories. They talked for a long time and Kenzie agreed to catch some birds for Slimbridge. In fact he later netted and dispatched thirty-two male pinkfeet, seventeen pinkfeet he couldn't sex, thirty-one females, forty-seven brent, twelve wigeon, five shelduck, one pintail and one barnacle goose.

At the end of each season Kenzie reported to Scott the numbers of the rings taken from birds he had shot. From time to time Kenzie received letters from Scott about these matters. One, signed "Peter", arrived in December 1952. This letter thanked Kenzie for sending Scott details of ringed geese shot during the season, and went on to give an account of a wildfowling expedition Scott had just enjoyed in Ireland.

"I had a wonderful day on the Wexford Slob," wrote Scott, "and shot eighteen Greenland whitefronts. The geese behave quite differently there, and split up into small parties unlike the pinkfeet on the Wash."

Next year came the letter that suggested Kenzie stop shooting geese.

"After having had a record season," suggested Scott, "you really ought to give the geese a rest. People won't think the better of you if you slaughter geese wholesale over decoys. Besides—like me—you've shot enough geese now. Why not let them off for a bit? You must have found, as I did, that when you get too good at it, it's too easy, and not much fun any more."

Kenzie's reaction was predictable. It was this: "Last year he wrote to me and told me that he'd shot eighteen Greenland whitefronts in Ireland, and now, after all the geese he's shot, he's telling me to pack it up. I should say so."

Next season he accounted for 150 geese.

Kenzie scanning the winter fields in 1976.
Photo by courtesy of Don Andrew.

If Kenzie could not work at Slimbridge he could at least have a Wildfowl Trust of his own.

The Thorpes live in a council house, in a street of small neat houses in Sutton Bridge. Their house looks the same as all the others until you walk round the back. No dogs bark at you, for Kenzie has not used a gundog for some years. Instead a cock wigeon whistles and a pinkfoot gander gobbles. You see that the whole of the small back garden has been enclosed with wire to make a giant aviary. At the far end are bales of straw.

Close to the house is a miniature pond and around it an area of clean, carefully raked gravel. A pair of teal are upending in the pond. Mallard, shelduck, wigeon, a gadwall and pintail are dozing in the grass. Eight geese, including two pairs of pinkfeet and a whitefront gander are picking grains of wheat from between the stones. Most of the birds were caught by Kenzie or found wounded or pricked by shot on the marsh. One pinkfoot he picked up with a torch at night on a poaching expedition in 1949. Another was caught in a flight-net at Drove End. A third was recovered wounded in 1954. One at least has been away on migration and returned, though, alas, the neighbours became so excited as it circled the chimney pots that it took fright and did not stay.

The whole aviary is bizarre in its setting and in every way extraordinary. It does not, however, mean that its custodian has had second thoughts about shooting, for it is a fact inconceivable to sentimentalists that many practical naturalists are also sportsmen, and it is part of the ambivalence of the wildfowler especially both to revere his quarry and to pursue it.

There are other signs, however, that Mackenzie Thorpe may one day cease to shoot so many geese, for he has acquired a cine-camera, and photography is a well-known and well-trodden path to conversion. So perhaps he means it when he says: "One day I shall give up shooting the geese and only shoot pigeons." But I do not care to forecast when that day might be.

I believe that Mackenzie Thorpe is one of the most successful men I know. He has done that very rare thing—managed to make a living at something which, anyway, he would do for the sport. As he said to his brother Bob when the other complained of exhaustion on an early wild goose chase: "It's the sport, man." What is more astonishing is that he has achieved all this in the open air, independent for the most part of employers, and at a time when the motor-car, the caravan, the transistor radio and the sheer pressure of population threaten to make an urbanized slum of the countryside. He has just, but only just, got his life in in time.

Kenzie has absorbed some worthwhile things from that other, largely city-bred, world he had taken out shooting, but he has managed to remain reasonably uncontaminated. I hope he remains so and never becomes a professional "character". Schooling passed him by, a fact which reveals itself when you get a letter from him. Properly educated he might have gone further—in some people's estimation anyway—but who can say in what direction. I have already made the point that he is an original, and there are few enough of those about. What matter if an original can't spell? Anyway, he has now returned to his school as a local celebrity, for some of his by no means mediocre paintings hang in the Sutton Bridge schoolrooms where once he was the bad boy of the few forms through which he managed to progress.

I leave the last words to him:

"Looking back on my shooting, it has never been the stuff that I've got that has mattered. It's always been the thrill of moving in and out of the trees and bushes, of crossing the fences and dykes and going down the marsh in the darkness, and the excitement of never knowing what might happen next.

"Take my poaching. You never get rich by poaching. You never hear of poachers retiring. But in poaching and wildfowling it's always the fun of doing something you know no one else can do as well, and very few can do at all. These people who shoot ladidadi don't know what they're missing. To poach a thing is better than having permission to go on the land. The same with goose shooting. Outwitting one wild goose is better than bagging a thousand driven pheasants.

"I've given up the poaching business now and one day I may give up wildfowling. But there've been times when it's been snowing and blowing that I've been singing at the top of my voice in the darkness because I knew no one else was up and no one could hear me. I've thoroughly enjoyed every moment of it, and if I had my time to come I'd do it all again, just the same. Just exactly the same."